THE
GOSPEL
FOR LIFE

THE GOSPEL &

Same-Sex
Marriage

THE
GOSPEL
FOR LIFE

——— SERIES ———

THE GOSPEL &

Same-Sex
Marriage

SERIES EDITORS

RUSSELL MOORE *and*

ANDREW T. WALKER

PUBLISHING GROUP

NASHVILLE, TENNESSEE

978-1-4336-9049-5

Published by B&H Publishing Group
Nashville, Tennessee

Dewey Decimal Classification: 306.84
Subject Heading: GOSPEL \ SAME-SEX MARRIAGE \
HOMOSEXUALITY

1 2 3 4 5 6 7 8 • 21 20 19 18 17 16

CONTENTS

Series Preface

Russell Moore

Why Should *The Gospel for Life* Series Matter to Churches?

IN ACTS CHAPTER 2, WE READ ABOUT THE DAY OF PENTECOST, the day when the resurrected Lord Jesus sent the Holy Spirit. The Day of Pentecost was a spectacular day—there were manifestations of fire, languages being spoken by people who didn't know them, and thousands of unbelievers coming to faith in this recently resurrected Messiah. Reading this passage, we go from account to account of heavenly shock and awe, and yet the passage ends in an unexpectedly simple way: "And they devoted themselves to the apostles' teaching and the fellowship, to the breaking of bread and the prayers" (Acts 2:42).

I believe one thing the Holy Spirit wants us to understand from this is that these "ordinary" things are not less miraculous than what preceded them—in fact, they may be more so. The disciplines of discipleship, fellowship, community, and prayer are the signs that tell us the kingdom of Christ is here. That means that for Christians, the most crucial moments in our walk with Jesus Christ don't happen in the thrill of "spiritual highs." They happen in the common hum of everyday life in quiet, faithful obedience to Christ.

That's what *The Gospel for Life* series is about: taking the truths of Scripture, the story of our redemption and adoption by a risen Lord Jesus, and applying them to the questions and situations that we all face in the ordinary course of life.

Our hope is that churches will not merely find these books interesting, but also helpful. *The Gospel for Life* series is meant to assist pastors and church leaders to answer urgent questions that people are asking, questions that the church isn't always immediately ready to answer. Whether in a counseling session or alongside a sermon series, these books are intended to come alongside church leaders in discipling members to see their lives with a Kingdom mentality.

Believers don't live the Christian life in isolation but rather as part of a gospel community, the church. That's why we have structured *The Gospel for Life* series to be easily utilized in anything from a small group study context to a new member or new believer class. None of us can live worthy of the gospel by ourselves and, thankfully, none have to.

Why are we so preoccupied with the idea of living life by and through the gospel? The answer is actually quite simple: because the gospel changes everything. The gospel isn't a mere theological system or a political idea, though it shapes both our theology and our politics. The gospel is the Good News that there is a Kingdom far above and beyond the borders of this world, where death is dead and sin and sorrow cease. The gospel is about how God brings this Kingdom to us by reconciling us to Himself through Christ.

That means two things. First, it means the gospel fulfills the hopes that our idols have promised and betrayed. The Scripture says that all God's promises are yes in Jesus (2 Cor. 1:20). As sinful human beings, we all tend to think what we really want is freedom from authority, inheritance without obedience like the prodigal son. But what Jesus offers is the authority we were designed to live under, an inheritance we by no means deserve to share, and the freedom that truly satisfies our souls.

Second, this means that the gospel isn't just the start of the Christian life but rather the vehicle that carries it along. The gospel is about the daily reality of living as an adopted child of a resurrected Father-King, whose Kingdom is here and is still coming. By looking at our jobs, our marriages, our families, our government, and the entire universe through a gospel lens, we live differently. We will work and marry and vote with a Kingdom mind-set, one that prioritizes the permanent things of

Christ above the fleeting pleasures of sin and the vaporous things of this world.

The Gospel for Life series is about helping Christians and churches navigate life in the Kingdom while we wait for the return of its King and its ultimate consummation. The stakes are high. To get the gospel wrong when it comes to marriage can lead to a generation's worth of confusion about what marriage even is. To get the gospel wrong on adoption can leave millions of "unwanted" children at the mercy of ruthless sex traffickers and callous abusers. There's no safe space in the universe where getting the gospel wrong will be merely an academic blunder. That's why these books exist—to help you and your church understand what the gospel is and what it means for life.

Theology doesn't just think; it walks, weeps, and bleeds. *The Gospel for Life* series is a resource intended to help Christians see their theology do just that. When you see all of life from the perspective of the Kingdom, everything changes. It's not just about miraculous moments or intense religious experiences. Our gospel is indeed miraculous, but as the disciples in Acts learned, it's also a gospel of the ordinary.

Introduction

Andrew T. Walker

AMERICAN CHRISTIANS NOW FIND THEMSELVES AT A PLACE that, in the year 2000, would seem inconceivable: same-sex marriage is now legal in all fifty states. The growing acceptance, normalization, and celebration of homosexuality is one of the fastest social movements in American history. Many Christians find themselves perplexed as to how we got to where we are today. Others feel disappointment that our nation has redefined marriage to include a practice that the Bible and Christian history have all regarded as sinful. It seems that with same-sex marriage, Christianity's place in culture grows more dim and estranged from the culture around it.

Same-sex marriage will represent the greatest point of conflict that Christians will have in culture for the foreseeable future. It will fracture Christian denominations. Agreements and disagreements will sever friendships. It will divide families. Employees who feel alienated by a work environment

1

that celebrates homosexuality and same-sex marriage will feel increasingly alienated. Times are going to be hard. If supporters of same-sex marriage regard it as a matter of basic justice and fairness, and Christians regard it as a matter of sin and contrary to human flourishing, conflict is bound to occur. It's important, then, to understand what the nature of the disagreement is; for the discussion pertaining to sexuality and marriage pertains to almost every area of life: education, entertainment, the media, and politics.

But Christians can't give up. A church that faces cultural exile will not be, nor ever should it be, a church in retreat. We've been here before. From the ashes of a smoldering Roman Empire, the Christian church emerged out of a culture more hostile to the Christian gospel than even our own. The beauty of Christian doctrine will win out, even though in the short term it may feel like we're losing. Throughout this, we have to remember to "guard the good deposit" (2 Tim. 1:14) of faith entrusted to us, which means guarding the richly beautiful doctrine of Christian marriage.

To understand how significant marriage is, is to understand how God purposefully made us male and female. He did not make us "Spouse A" and "Spouse B." Rather, in the richness of our being made male and female, God made men and women uniquely fit for marriage. From this union, God designed children to be created. In this beautiful institution given to all of creation, the apostle Paul says that marriage somehow mysteriously reflects the deepest truth of the cosmos: the Christ-church union (Eph. 5:21–33). So, despite whatever cultural moment we're in, we can't give up on marriage because we don't have the authority to give up on marriage. Jesus said marriage is "from the beginning" (Matt. 19:4). If Jesus said marriage is "from the beginning," it also means, according to Jesus, that it has a future. That future has been dealt to us and it beckons us to be faithful.

Each book in *The Gospel for Life* series is structured the same: What are we for? What does the gospel say? How should the Christian live? How should the church engage? What does the culture say?

The Gospel & Same-Sex Marriage is intended to be an introductory look at how Christians should engage this most controversial topic from every angle of the Christian's life—their place in culture, their engagement as everyday Christians, and their role in the body of Christ, the church. We want no stone unturned when talking about how the gospel of Jesus Christ shapes us as a people on mission for God. So, on the issue of same-sex marriage, we've assembled cultural experts, theologians, and pastors to help equip us as Christians on the issue of same-sex marriage.

Our hope is that after reading this book, you'll feel encouraged and equipped to engage this sensitive subject with your friends and family; that you'll be able to articulate what marriage is, its importance to society, and how Christians should go about proclaiming this truth of marriage in a culture that seems further and further removed from marriage altogether.

CHAPTER

1

What Are We For?

Andrew T. Walker

THERE'S ALWAYS A LOT OF EVANGELICAL ANGST AND DISCOMFORT about our tendency to be *against* some things more than we are *for* other things. If you take this line of thought, evangelical Christians are often depicted as oppositional by nature, eagerly looking to knock down any and every newfound cultural concept that doesn't align with Scripture. Our critics accuse us of this mind-set, which leads to a growing self-awareness that evangelical identity shouldn't be grounded merely in what we reject, but what we should contribute to, cultivate, and promote.

In order to answer the question, "What are we for?" in regards to marriage debates in our culture, we need to define who "we" are and to what moral authority we are accountable. We are Christians who belong to the church of Jesus Christ, Christians who are ruled by God's Word. We are those who believe the Bible is inspired, inerrant, infallible, sufficient, and clear. The Bible is God's Word. And we are those who believe God gets the final word on marriage and sexuality.

The Bible is unambiguously clear about marriage's definition and purpose. So, the opportunity to be *for* something is what the Bible gives to us when talking about marriage. The Bible's witness on marriage doesn't allow for same-sex marriage, not because the Bible gives attention to same-sex marriage, but because the biblical narrative on marriage doesn't conceive of same-sex marriage as within the realm of possibility.

Using the Bible to advocate for same-sex marriage is akin to using the Bible to advocate for using surf boards as a mode of transportation on interstate highways: The Bible doesn't give footing to any categories that it doesn't recognize.

The Bible is silent on offering any constructive case for same-sex marriage because the Bible's definition of marriage prohibits the very concept of same-sex marriage. Looking at all that the Bible says on marriage, same-sex marriage simply isn't fathomable without contorting and twisting the Bible beyond the bounds of reason. Even still, that hasn't stopped some individuals from suggesting that the Bible can be used to endorse same-sex relationships. We'll tackle those claims further on.

First, I want to argue that the Bible presents marriage as something fixed and unalterable given by God for the sake of creation and human fulfillment. Secondly, I'll discuss how marriage, in the Bible, is a shadow or image of the greatest truth of the universe: the gospel of Jesus Christ. Third, I want to argue that the Bible's definition of marriage is natural in the sense that its definition translates to people and cultures that are not distinctly Christian. Here, I'll discuss why marriage isn't just a private institution, but a public institution. In the field of ethics, we call this a natural law argument, since it's an argument believed to be universally valid and known across all cultures.[1] When we're finished, we'll see why same-sex marriage fails to satisfy the criteria of what properly constitutes a marriage according to the Bible.

Marriage by Design

The most basic and significant place to begin discussing marriage is the beginning of marriage itself—at Creation.

Assigned as ruler and caretaker of the Garden of Eden, Adam was to "have dominion over the fish of the sea and over the birds of the heavens and over the livestock and over all the earth and over every creeping thing that creeps on the earth" (Gen. 1:26). He told Adam: "Be fruitful and multiply and fill the earth and subdue it, and have dominion over the fish of the sea and over the birds of the heavens and over every living thing that moves on the earth" (Gen. 1:28).

Adam found himself without an adequate counterpart that would help share in the mission God had given him (Gen. 2:20). Even in a sinless state, God declared that it was not good that Adam should be alone (Gen. 2:18); and so from Adam, but different than Adam, God knit together the perfect counterpart for him—a woman. They were alike in their humanity, but different in their design. But this difference is a complementary difference. Male and female difference contributes to the overall betterment of the pair. Think of a tongue and groove joint and how the pieces, though designed differently, when put together, form something new.

From this differentiated pair, a divine spark went forth from them, a spark that only a man and woman can unite to fulfill: "a man shall leave his father and his mother and hold fast to his wife, and they shall become one flesh" (Gen. 2:24). The "one flesh" symbolism is a powerful metaphor for how profound the union is of a man and woman. Man and woman fit together in a way unique to their complementary design. This simple story captures the essence of every human society; for at the foundation of every society is the union of one man and one woman. For from man and woman comes the only possibility for the continuation of mission and society through the bearing of children.

From the biblical narrative, we see the definition of marriage take a shape. God designed a man and a woman to become a husband and a wife so that they might become a father and mother to any children their union produces. A marriage forms when a man and woman join together in a permanent union for the purposes of building a family. The emphasis on procreation is important. Were man and woman not capable of reproducing, it is questionable whether marriage would be an institution ever conceived of by God. The very fact of procreation makes marriage exclusive to men and woman alone.

The simplicity of the marital structure is of supreme importance. Take note that Adam and Eve's union is a gendered and *complementary* union, which means it consists of a man and woman whose anatomical structure is designed, literally, to fit together for the creation of offspring. This is very important, because many advocates for same-sex marriage must downplay or altogether remove the male-female complementarity to argue for same-sex marriage.

Also observe that the marriage union of a man and woman consists of just one man and one woman, making their marital union *monogamous* (married only to one another). Sadly, as Israel deviates from God's divine mission, their leaders and its people begin taking on multiple wives, thwarting God's intention that marriage be reserved for only one man and one woman. Adam and Eve were to be sexually *exclusive* (having sexual relations only with one another).

And nowhere in the narrative is the union of Adam and Eve assumed to be anything other than *permanent*, meaning that their union was to persist throughout the duration of their lives. When you enter marriage, marriage is assumed to be lifelong.

What Marriage Is

"A thing is a thing, not what is said of that thing."[2]

Complementary. Monogamy. Exclusivity. Permanency. Here we see the structure of marriage take shape in final form according to the Bible. But what does "structure" mean? For something to have a structure means that it has a definite composition. And were one of the elements that make up the structure removed, you would no longer persist in having the original structure.

An illustration from chemistry class might help explain this in greater detail. Think of the atomical structure of water: H_2O. Water *is* something. If we take away either a hydrogen molecule or an oxygen molecule, water will cease to exist. Now, perhaps a creative individual might want to add an additional oxygen molecule and call the resulting structure "water," but any person who knows what water is—or who has experienced the quenching effects that only water can give—will know that just calling something by an original name does not, in fact, make it the original thing.

The same is true for marriage. Marriage *is* something. Once marriage is redefined as no longer complementary, the whole matrix of marriage's foundation collapses. If marriage is no longer complementary, why must it be permanent? And if marriage is no longer permanent, why must it be exclusive? Why is the number two so important to retain if marriage is no longer complementary? Marriage revisionists refuse to answer these questions beyond saying such questions are a "slippery slope," but I've not yet heard any satisfying answers on why redefining marriage wouldn't logically lead to these possibilities.

From the foundation of the complementarity of the man and the woman springs the shape of marriage itself. If the complementary basis of marriage as man and woman is removed, the other strands that make up marriage become arbitrary and endlessly subjective.

What Marriage Is Not

This is why the advent of same-sex marriage is, slowly, bringing with it entirely new paradigms for human relationships, all of which chip away at the trust, beauty, and sanctity that biblical marriage promises. One lawyer in a prominent, elite newspaper suggested that marriage should be term-limited and renewable after an allotted period of time. He called the arrangement a "wedlease."[3]

A popular writer, Dan Savage, wrote that monogamy is simply unrealistic, and so he created the novel term *monogamish* to suggest that spouses could have multiple sex partners as long as it happened in an open, honest atmosphere where the other spouse knew such actions were happening and were not hiding anything from one another.[4]

New York Magazine introduced a word into the American vocabulary when it wrote of a three-person couple—a "throuple"—that lived together as a sexual triad.[5]

The contrast to this always-changing, always-adapting understanding of marriage is to view marriage as the Bible, history, and civilization always has: as complementary, unalterable, and oriented toward the care of children, not simply the erotic desires of adults. According to marriage scholar Ryan T. Anderson:

> Marriage, rightly understood, brings together the two halves of humanity (male and female) in a monogamous relationship. Through vows of permanence and exclusivity, husband and wife pledge to each other to be faithful. Marriage gives to children a relationship with the man and the woman who made them, their mom and dad.[6]

Many will often say that Jesus was silent on the topic of homosexuality or same-sex marriage. This is patently false. Jesus reaffirmed the creational account of marriage in Matthew 19:4–6. His words bear repeating in full:

> He answered, "Have you not read that he who created them from the beginning made them male and female, and said, 'Therefore a man shall leave his father and his mother and hold fast to his wife, and the two shall become one flesh'? So they are no longer two but one flesh. What therefore God has joined together, let not man separate."

What did Jesus do in this passage? He reaffirmed the truthfulness of Genesis 1 and 2. He reaffirmed the shape of marriage as being limited to one man and one woman. He reaffirmed the permanency and exclusivity of the marital bond.

By echoing the "one flesh" union of Genesis 2, Jesus is putting the purpose of marriage on full display: that men and women unite comprehensively together in marriage through a physical, spiritual, and emotional bond that is oriented to and fulfilled by the creation and rearing of children.

It is worth noting that the definition of marriage as discussed here is not simply unique to Christianity or the Bible. Marriage is *ultimately* Christian because God created it, but it isn't *exclusive to* Christians right now, since God designed marriage to be available to all of creation. Countless civilizations going back as far as human history has record—some of them very irreligious—have all held special regard for the union of one man and one woman because they understood that only one type of relationship sprang forth children. Diverse cultures and ancient philosophers who had little exposure to religion such as Socrates, Plato, Aristotle, and Plutarch all reached the same conclusion about marriage.[7] As the authors of *What Is Marriage?* note, "This suggests only that no one religion invented marriage. It is rather marriage—the demands of the natural institution—that has helped to shape our religious and philosophical traditions."[8]

What Has God Revealed to Us About Marriage?

As we saw above, marriage is a creational institution ordained by God meant for the furtherance of the human race, the stability of society, and the satisfaction of deep longing for relationship and intimacy that exists between men and women.

But marriage is chiefly about the glory of God (1 Cor. 6:16–20). We might say that marriage's purpose exists on two levels. First, it's a human institution intricately woven into the nature of existence and human civilization. Second, in the Bible, marriage is depicted as an earthly shadow of the most important truth of the universe: the gospel of Jesus Christ.

Pay close attention to Paul's words in Ephesians 5:

> Wives, submit to your own husbands, as to the Lord.
> For the husband is the head of the wife even as Christ
> is the head of the church, his body, and is himself its
> Savior. Now as the church submits to Christ, so also
> wives should submit in everything to their husbands.
>
> Husbands, love your wives, as Christ loved the
> church and gave himself up for her, that he might
> sanctify her, having cleansed her by the washing
> of water with the word, so that he might present
> the church to himself in splendor, without spot or
> wrinkle or any such thing, that she might be holy and
> without blemish. In the same way husbands should
> love their wives as their own bodies. He who loves
> his wife loves himself. For no one ever hated his own
> flesh, but nourishes and cherishes it, just as Christ
> does the church, because we are members of his body.
> "Therefore a man shall leave his father and mother
> and hold fast to his wife, and the two shall become
> one flesh." This mystery is profound, and I am saying
> that it refers to Christ and the church. However, let
> each one of you love his wife as himself, and let the
> wife see that she respects her husband. (vv. 22–33)

In Ephesians, the apostle Paul speaks of "mystery" several times throughout the book. The "mystery" according to Paul, is God's act "to unite all things in him, things in heaven and things on earth" (Eph. 1:9–10). Paul reveals that marriage, too, is a "mystery" that somehow communicates the message of the gospel of Christ crucified and risen for sinners (Rom. 3:21–26; 1 Cor. 15:3–4; 1 Thess. 5:9–10). He uses marital imagery to evoke the act of reconciliation that occurs in the gospel.

This has profound ramifications for the biblical understanding of marriage as something more than just creational. According to the Bible, God's action in designing the complementarity of marriage is purposeful and meant to direct our gaze upon Jesus and all that He has done to redeem his bride, the church. As Russell Moore notes regarding Paul's use of "mystery" throughout Ephesians, "One key aspect of this unveiled mystery is that the family structure is not an arbitrary expression of nature or of the will of God. Marriage and family are instead archetypes, icons of God's purposes for the universe."[9]

Additionally, in the book of Revelation, John writes that:

> Then I heard what seemed to be the voice of a great multitude, like the roar of many waters and like the sound of mighty peals of thunder, crying out,
>
> > "Hallelujah!
> > For the Lord our God the Almighty reigns.

Let us rejoice and exult
     and give him the glory,
for the marriage of the Lamb has come,
     and his Bride has made herself ready;
it was granted her to clothe herself
     with fine linen, bright and pure"—
for the fine linen is the righteous deeds of the saints.

And the angel said to me, "Write this: Blessed are
those who are invited to the marriage supper of the
Lamb." And he said to me, "These are the true words
of God." (Rev. 19:6–9)

In the strongest terms possible, the climax of history is communicated in marital imagery. What this communicates is that earthly marriage is a shadow, awaiting fulfillment of a heavenly marriage of God and His redeemed.

The Bible and Marriage's Purposes

So far, we've discussed how marriage is rooted in Creation and finds its climax in the story of the gospel. But what about the "traditional" or biblical view of marriage as a public policy issue? Is there a biblical reason for why marriage should continue to be viewed only between one man and one woman on a societal level? This is an important question, because there are some Christians who insist that the state should remove itself from within the sphere of marriage altogether. Often with good intentions, some Christians wish to privatize marriage into a strictly ecclesial practice, treating it like we would the Lord's Supper or baptism.

While marriage is certainly of concern to the church, it has a scope of consequence that goes beyond just the four walls of a church. By definition, marriage is a public institution, which means it serves the public good by helping facilitate access to the common good. In other words, marriage is for everyone—not just Christians. There are many good reasons for why the state should continue to uphold the biblical definition of marriage.

What Is the Government's Role in Marriage?

The government, rightly, is not in the business of upholding theological positions or supporting one religion's code of ethics over another. The government forbids stealing, for example, not simply because the Ten Commandments forbid it, but because stealing undermines cooperation and trust in our everyday lives. Because stealing undermines cooperation, common belief about the harms of theft leads to outlawing it. Of course, as Christians, we believe everything has God as its author, and so we view stealing as breaking God's commandment. But that is not government's interest in making theft illegal. The same is true for marriage. I don't expect the government to acknowledge that marriage is ultimately anchored in the truth of the gospel. But I do expect the government to uphold a view of marriage that is necessary for uniting men, women, and children together for the sake of child well-being and social harmony. When we advocate for marriage in the public square, we do so as Christians, but we do so not because marriage serves the interests just of the Christian community, but of the wider community—non-Christians and all. It cannot be stressed how important it is to remember that the picture of marriage given at creation is a testament to marriage's importance to *all* of creation.

One of the biggest reasons is that marriage serves as the most natural institution that naturally binds men, women, and children together. For this reason, it is actually impossible for the state to be neutral to marriage, because citizens come together in romantic ways and from that, children often spring. Commissioned to be an institution that pursues justice (Rom. 13:1–4), the state has an active interest in seeing its tiniest, most vulnerable, and dependent citizens—children—cared for. Children have a right to a mother and father; and a proper definition of marriage helps ensure that children will grow up with a mother and father. A government is more just when it recognizes that marriage is something that the government recognizes, not creates.

When a child is born, biology tells us that a mother will always be nearby. Will the father?[10] Sadly, in American culture, marriage has fallen by the wayside and skyrocketing rates of out-of-wedlock childbearing have occurred. Children born outside of marriage face a much higher risk of experiencing poverty at some point in their life. When the state supports the correct definition, and when this definition is respected throughout broader culture, it works to reinforce moral norms that place responsibility for parenting between both the man and woman who created the child.

What Is the Church's Role in Marriage?

The Bible demands and social science suggests that children require both a mom and dad in order to be fully prepared for the demands of life. When the state properly defines marriage, it helps ensure that its citizens enter life with every opportunity and relationship necessary for he or she to flourish. While there is not one particular biblical verse to support this claim, ensuring that government does not overstep its bounds and redefines marriage fits within the broader biblical definition of what constitutes God's intention for just government.

It's true, anyone can benefit from the good of marriage—whether they are a Christian or not. Society flourishes when marriage policies align with God's design for marriage (complementary, monogamy, exclusivity, permanency). Churches have a unique opportunity to witness to the truth of marriage. Churches can petition their governing leaders to stand true to marriage. Pastors can teach on marriage and, in turn, help form the conscience on what marriage is and why it matters to individuals within the church. Christians ought to stand firm in the truth that marriages are strongest when they seek to align themselves, not only in cooperation with government policy on marriage, but in submission to the authority of a local church. Local churches that submit themselves to Christ enable marriages to thrive in the context of Christian community, a benefit that enhances marriages and shines a light on the mysterious image of Christ and His church illustrated by its nature (Eph. 5).

Local churches offer marital support in community (upholding marriage's permanency). The church helps couples imagine life together to build relationships together for mutual benefit (casting vision for why complementarity matters). The church encourages sexual intimacy and holds members accountable—through biblical church discipline—who violate Christian sexual ethics (upholding marriage's monogamous and exclusive nature). In sum, while the state *compels* all citizens to obey marriage policies by law for their own good, the church is the place that God's people come together *voluntarily* to submit to God's laws for the benefit of their own good.

Responding to the Revisionists[11]

Sadly, today, there are self-proclaimed Christians who advocate for same-sex marriage. Amounting to little more than biblical revisionists who desire to bend the Scripture to excuse their sin, those who do so under the banner of Christian teaching are false teachers and should be rebutted (Matt. 7:15; 2 John 1:10–11; 2 Pet. 2:1–22). Differences about the purposes of human sexuality are not matters of amiable disagreement, but about matters of eternal destiny (1 Cor. 6:9–11). Christians who insist upon the legitimacy of same-sex marriage are preaching a false gospel.

Their arguments come in many shapes and forms, but they can be summarized briefly as follows:

1. Christian teaching on homosexuality and marriage has produced harm in the lives of homosexuals.
2. The world of the Bible does not speak to the issue of a modern and comprehensive understanding of sexual orientation.
3. The Bible speaks without any reference to the modern knowledge of faithful, loving, and committed same-sex couples.
4. The patriarchal context within the world of the Bible explains the prohibitions against homosexuality.

Though space prevents going in-depth about the types of arguments that biblical revisionists make to endorse same-sex relationships and same-sex marriage, it becomes apparent from the start that these activists' basic thesis regarding sexual orientation and marriage is not derived from the text of Scripture. Rather, the force of their argument in favor of legitimizing homosexual desire and same-sex marriage is used to explain away the biblical text. They rely on some other authority for their basic claim—namely, a nonbiblical moral authority, that neither the history of scriptural interpretation nor church history considers valid. They do not appeal to the sound biblical interpretation, but rather use their own subjective understanding to bend the text to affirm their own interpretation. Their arguments are first a moral presupposition, followed by a belief that the Scriptures *could* affirm homosexuality and same-sex marriage based on the cavalier exegesis and theological interpretation they offer.

Jesus said marriage was from the beginning (Matt. 19:4–6). So neither we nor LGBT "Christian" activists have the authority to redefine marriage, or the biblical bounds of sexual relationships, or anything else that hits a cultural pressure point, any more than pseudo-evangelicals have the authority to redefine what the Evangel—the gospel—really is, which is what this is about. The Evangel isn't a message where people write their own script. The "Evangel" of evangelicalism offers new life, but also demands repentance. How is the Evangel good news if it doesn't offer freedom from sexual sin but instead baptizes it?

Conclusion

Marriage isn't just about children. But neither is marriage just about adult romance. It isn't just about deep emotional connection. Marriage is ultimately about the glory of God in the gospel. The gospel reigns supreme over our reflections on the nature of marriage. The very fact that this debate over the definition of marriage is so heated is a sign that all of us agree that marriage is different from many other relationships. In truth, marriage connects men, women, and children into one institution that society depends upon.

In no manner of honest interpretation can the legitimacy of same-sex marriage be developed from Scripture. To insist that the Scriptures give even tacit endorsement to the morality of homosexuality or the possibility of same-sex marriage is to dispense with a clear reading of the text and to discard thousands of years of church witness.

Let's conclude this chapter on the simplest of observations: What does the Bible say about same-sex marriage? Nothing. The Bible doesn't conceive of such an institution ever being a possibility. For one, the nature of same-sex marriage is based on sexual practices that the Bible considers sinful. Second, the scriptural purpose of marriage is something that same-sex marriage could never fulfill. Marriage is based in the complementarity of the sexes, and the very real possibility that marriage relationships produce children. Same-sex couples cannot, by definition, produce what society needs: children. This isn't to be harsh or critical of same-sex attracted persons in general. It is to communicate, however, that the nature of same-sex relationships are never marital, and thus not biblical in any imaginable scenario.

So, what are we for? We are for humanity flourishing in society as God designed, the church to flourish under God's rule, and for God's Kingdom to come on earth, as it is in heaven.

Discussion Questions

1. What is the Bible's definition of marriage? How do we get that definition?
2. Why is marriage important to all people, including those outside of the church? And why does same-sex marriage fail to live up to the standards of biblical marriage?
3. What is the role of government in marriage? What is the role of the church in fostering a healthy culture of marriage inside and outside of the church?

2

What Does the Gospel Say?

John Piper

LET THE MARRIAGE BED BE HELD IN HONOR.

Hebrews 13:1–6 says:

> Let brotherly love continue. Do not neglect to
> show hospitality to strangers, for thereby some have
> entertained angels unawares. Remember those who
> are in prison, as though in prison with them, and
> those who are mistreated, since you also are in the
> body. Let marriage be held in honor among all, and
> let the marriage bed be undefiled, for God will judge

the sexually immoral and adulterous. Keep your life free from love of money, and be content with what you have, for he has said, "I will never leave you nor forsake you." So we can confidently say, "The Lord is my helper; I will not fear; what can man do to me?"

This chapter is built around eight points designed to give a biblical vision of marriage in relationship to the sin of homosexuality and the offer of redemption through the gospel. I begin with Hebrews 13:1–6 not because I will give an exposition of it, but to highlight one phrase in verse 4: "Let marriage be held in honor among all." That is what I hope to advance, for the glory of God and for your guidance and your good.

Designed by God

Marriage is created and defined by God in the Scriptures as the sexual and covenantal union of a man and a woman in lifelong allegiance to each other alone, as husband and wife, with a view to displaying Christ's covenant relationship to his blood-bought church.

This is seen most clearly from four passages where these truths are woven together:

God created man in his own image, in the image of God he created him; male and female he created them. And God blessed them. And God said to

them, "Be fruitful and multiply and fill the earth."
(Gen. 1:27–28)

And then God linked his design in manhood and womanhood with marriage in Genesis 2:23–24. When the woman is
created from his side, the man exclaims:

> "This at last is bone of my bones and flesh of my
> flesh; she shall be called Woman, because she was
> taken out of Man." Therefore, a man shall leave his
> father and his mother and hold fast to his wife, and
> they shall become one flesh.

In other words, God created man male and female so that
there might be a one-flesh sexual union and covenantal cleaving
with a view to multiplying the human race, and displaying God's
covenant with His people, and eventually Christ's covenant with
His church.

Remarkably, Jesus picked up on this link between Creation
and marriage and lifelong covenant, weaving together these very
two texts from Genesis. All that the Old Testament affirms about
the uniqueness of marriage being singularly expressed through
one man and one woman, Jesus reaffirms:

> "Have you not read that he who created them from
> the beginning made them male and female [Gen.
> 1:27], and said [quoting Gen. 2:24], 'Therefore

[linking creation and marriage] a man shall leave his
father and his mother and hold fast to his wife, and
the two shall become one flesh'? So they are no longer
two but one flesh. What therefore God has joined
together, let not man separate." (Matt. 19:4–6)

And in our cultural setting, the words, "Let not man separate the male and female that God has joined together," has vastly
greater significance than anyone ever thought it would.

One more text on the meaning of marriage makes the dis-
tinction between male and female—husband and wife—cov-
enantally significant as a portrayal of Christ and the church.

Now as the church submits to Christ, so also wives
should submit in everything to their husbands.
Husbands, love your wives, as Christ loved the
church and gave himself up for her. . . . "Therefore
[quoting Genesis 2:24] a man shall leave his father
and mother and hold fast to his wife, and the two
shall become one flesh." This mystery is profound,
and I am saying that it refers to Christ and the
church. (Eph. 5:24–25, 31–32)

In other words, from the beginning there has been a mysterious and profound meaning to marriage. And Paul is now
opening that mystery. And it is this: *God made man male and
female with their distinctive feminine and masculine natures and*

their distinctive roles so that in marriage as husband and wife they could display Christ and the church. Marriage is designed to reflect the deepest truths of the gospel.

This means that the basic roles of wife and husband are not interchangeable. The husband displays the sacrificial love of Christ's headship, and the wife displays the submissive role of Christ's body. The mystery of marriage is that God had this double (of wife and husband) display in mind when He created man as male and female. Therefore, the profoundest reality in the universe underlies marriage as a covenantal union between a man and a woman.

No Such Thing as Same-Sex Marriage

There is no such thing as so-called same-sex marriage, and it would be wise not to call it that.

The point here is not only that so-called same-sex marriage *shouldn't* exist, but that it *doesn't* and it *can't*. Those who believe that God has spoken to us truthfully in the Bible should not concede that the committed, lifelong partnership and sexual relations of two men or two women is marriage. It isn't. God has created and defined marriage. And what He has joined together in that creation and that definition cannot be separated and still called marriage in God's eyes.

Brokenness and Sin

*Same-sex desires and same-sex orientation are part of our bro-
ken and disordered sexuality owing to God's subjection of the created
order to futility because of man's sin.*

In Genesis 3, we read about the catastrophic moment when
the first man and woman rebelled against God. The effects on
them and on the world are described in chapters 3 and 4, and
then illustrated in the sin-soaked and death-ridden history of the
Old Testament—indeed the history of the world.

The apostle Paul sums it up like this in Romans 8:20–21:

> The creation was subjected to futility, not willingly,
> but because of him who subjected it, in hope that
> the creation itself will be set free from its bondage to
> corruption and obtain the freedom of the glory of the
> children of God.

And we know from verse 23 that part of the creation that
was subjected to death and futility was our own bodies—and
he stresses, yes, the bodies of the redeemed. "And not only the
creation, but we ourselves, who have the first fruits of the Spirit,
groan inwardly as we wait eagerly for adoption as sons, the
redemption of our bodies" (Rom. 8:23).

I am arguing that same-sex desires and same-sex orientation
are in that category of groaning—waiting for the redemption of
our bodies. Which means they are in the same broad category with

all kinds of disordered bodies and minds and emotions. If we tried to make a list of the kinds of emotional and mental and physical brokenness of the human family, the list would be unending. And all of us are broken and disordered in different ways. All of us are bent to desire things in different degrees that we should not want. We are all disordered in our emotions, or minds, our bodies.

This is a call for careful distinctions lest you hurt people—or yourself—unnecessarily. All our disorders, all our brokenness, is rooted in sin—original sin and our sinful nature. It would be right to say that same-sex desires are sinful in the sense that they are disordered by sin and exist contrary to God's revealed will. But to be caused by sin and rooted in sin does not make a sinful desire equal to sinning. Sinning is what happens when rebellion against God expresses itself through our disorders.

Intercourse, Not Desire

Therefore, same-sex intercourse, not same-sex desire is the focus of Paul's condemnation when he threatens exclusion from the kingdom of God.

The clearest statement is found in 1 Corinthians 6:9–10.

> Do you not know that the unrighteous will not
> inherit the kingdom of God? Do not be deceived:
> neither the sexually immoral, nor idolaters, nor
> adulterers, nor men who practice homosexuality, nor

thieves, nor the greedy, nor drunkards, nor revilers,
nor swindlers will inherit the kingdom of God.

The words, "men who practice homosexuality" is a translation of two Greek words which refer to the passive and active partners in homosexual intercourse.[12] The focus is not on same-sex desire, but on same-sex practice. And notice that homosexual practice is not singled out but included with other ways of sinning: idolatry, adultery, stealing, greed, drunkenness, reviling, etc.

The point is not that one act of homosexual or heterosexual experimentation condemns you, but that returning to this lifestyle permanently and without repentance will condemn you. Men who practice—who give themselves over to this life, and do not repent—will not enter the kingdom of God. They will perish.

A Contradiction to Affirm

Therefore, it would contradict love and contradict the gospel of Jesus to approve homosexual practice, whether by silence, or by endorsing so-called same-sex marriage, or by affirming the Christian ordination of practicing homosexuals.

We must not be intimidated here. The world is going to say the opposite of what is true here. They are going to say that warning people who practice homosexuality about final judgment is hateful. It is not hateful. Hate does not want people to be saved. Hate does not want people to join the family. Hate wants to destroy. And sin does destroy. If homosexual practice (and greed and idolatry and reviling and drunkenness) leads to exclusion from the kingdom of God—as the Word of God says it does—then love warns. Love pleads. Love comes alongside and does all it can to help a person live—forever.

The Good News for Every Sinner

The good news of Jesus is that God saves heterosexual sinners and homosexual sinners who trust Jesus, by counting them righteous because of Christ, and by helping them through His Spirit to live lives pleasing to Him in their disordered brokenness.

After warning the Corinthians not to fall back into lives of sinful practice, Paul says this in 1 Corinthians 6:11, "And such were some of you. But you were washed, you were sanctified, you were justified in the name of the Lord Jesus Christ and by the Spirit of our God."

This is the heart of biblical Christianity. "Such were some of you." There were Christians in the church at Corinth who were fornicators and adulterers and thieves and drunkards and "men who practiced homosexuality." They were not driven away. They were folded in.

And the way they were folded in was that they were "justified in the name of the Lord Jesus Christ." That is, they put their trust in Jesus, they turned from their practice, they renounced sinful pursuit of their desires, and God justified them—He imputed to them the righteousness of Christ, and counted them as acceptable in His sight, and adopted them into His family—our family.

They were washed. That is, God took away all their guilt and shame. "He [Christ] himself bore our sins in his body on the tree, that we might die to sin and live to righteousness" (1 Pet. 2:24). So when they trusted Christ, all that He did counted for them, their sins were washed away.

And then they were "sanctified"—God set them apart for Himself and gave them His Spirit and was working in them a power for holiness that would swallow up their disordered desires in something greater and more beautiful and more desirable so that they could walk in a way pleasing to God, even in their brokenness.

The heart of Christianity is that God saves sinners through the death and resurrection of Jesus Christ. The best news in all the world is that Jesus Christ died and rose again so that the most bizarre sexual predator—homosexual or heterosexual—can be rescued from his path of destruction, washed, justified, sanctified, and given a place in God's all-satisfying presence by faith in Jesus Christ. This is the heart of our message.

How to Be a Faithful Citizen

Deciding what actions will be made legal or illegal through civil law is a moral activity aiming at the public good and informed by the worldview of each participant.

How should Christian citizens decide which of their views they should seek to put into law? Which moral convictions should Christians seek to pass as legal requirements?

Christians believe it is immoral to covet and to steal. But we seek to pass laws against stealing, not against coveting. One of the principles at work here seems to be that the line connecting coveting with damage to the public good is not clear enough. No doubt there is such a connection. God can see it and the public good would, we believe, be greatly enhanced if covetousness were overcome. But finite humans can't see it clearly enough to regulate coveting with laws and penalties. This is why we have to leave hundreds of immoral acts for Jesus to sort out when He comes.

Laws exist to preserve and enhance the public good. Which means that all laws are based on some conception of what is good for us. Which means that all legislation and all voting is a moral activity. It is based on choices about what is good for the public. And those choices are always informed by a worldview. And in that worldview—whether conscious or not—there are views of ultimate reality that determine what a person thinks the public good is.

Which means that all legislation is the legislation of morality. Someone's view of what is good—what is moral—wins the minds of the majority and carries the day. The question is: Which actions hurt the common good or enhance the common good so much that the one should be prohibited by law and the other should be required by law?

Here are a few thoughts to help you with that question:

The recognition of so-called same-sex marriage would be a clear social statement that motherhood or fatherhood or both are negligible in the public good of raising children. Two men adopting children cannot provide motherhood. And two women adopting children cannot provide fatherhood. But God ordained from the beginning that children grow up with a mother and a father, and said, "Honor your father and your mother" (Exod. 20:12). Tragedies in life often make that impossible. But taking actions to make that tragedy normal may be worth prohibiting by law. That's a factor to consider.

Marriage is the most fundamental institution among humans. Its origin is in the mind of God, and its beginning was at the beginning of the Creation of humankind. Its connections with all other parts of society are innumerable. Pretending that it can exist between people of the same sex will send ripple effects of dysfunction and destruction in every direction, most of which are now unforeseen. And many of those that are foreseen are tragic, especially for children, who will then produce a society we cannot now imagine.

Before now, as far as we know, no society in the history of the world has ever defined marriage as between people of the same sex. It is a mind-boggling innovation with no precedent to guide us, except the knowledge that unrighteousness destroys nations, and the celebration of it hastens the demise (Deut. 9:5; Prov. 13:34; Rom. 1:24–32).

How to Be a Faithful Member of the Body

Don't press the organization of the church or her pastors into political activism. Pray that the church and her ministers would feed the flock of God with the Word of God centered on the gospel of Christ crucified and risen. Expect from your shepherds not that they would rally you behind political candidates or legislative initiatives, but they would point you over and over again to God and to His Word, and to the cross.

Please try to understand this: *When I warn against the politicizing of the church, I do so not to diminish her power but to increase it.* The impact of the church for the glory of Christ and the good of the world does not increase when she shifts her priorities from the worship of God and the winning of souls and the nurturing of faith and raising up of new generations of disciples.

If the whole counsel of God is preached with power week in and week out, Christians who are citizens of heaven and citizens of this democratic order will be energized as they ought to speak and act for the common good.

Marvin Olasky expresses this well:

> Wise pastors prompt [Christians] to form associations outside the church, and leave the church to

its central task from which so many blessings flow. That pattern in the 18th and 19th centuries worked exceptionally well. New England pastors in colonial times preached and taught what the Bible said about liberty, and the Sons of Liberty—not a subset of any particular church—eventually sponsored a tea party in Boston harbor. Pastors through America during those centuries preached about biblical poverty-fighting, and in city after city Christians formed organizations such as (in New York) the Association for Improving the Condition of the Poor.[13]

Remember, you who trust in Jesus, "You were washed, you were sanctified, you were justified in the name of the Lord Jesus Christ and by the Spirit of our God" (1 Cor. 6:11). Be amazed that you are saved. And offer this to everyone.

Discussion Questions

1. What does the gospel communicate to someone with broken and sinful sexual desires?
2. How should Christians treat those with same-sex attraction?
3. How should the church communicate the gospel and marriage in the midst of upholding the social truth about marriage's importance?

3

How Should the Christian Live?

Jason G. Duesing

AT THE OUTBREAK OF WORLD WAR II WITH THE IMMINENT threat of German attack felt by many Londoners, the British government sought to inspire and instruct their citizens in their plight of endurance. To avoid paralysis of daily activity or mass hysteria caused by an avalanche of anxiety, the leaders propagated a sloganeering campaign. Perhaps the most popular slogan, however, was "Keep Calm and Carry On" as it resonated well with the stiff-upper-lip constitution of many Britons.[14] The idea of self-reinforced statements to bolster courage and focus energy, especially in the face of danger, is noble and proven effective for wartime morale or even sporting arena triumph. However, for the Christian, the temptation to anchor one's daily faith to self-reinforcement tactics can prove dangerous.

Thus, as the notion of same-sex marriage rapidly becomes normalized either in rhetoric or in law, how should the Christian live? Is it time to merely practice our stiff upper lip and "Keep Calm and Carry On"? Should we circle the wagons of paranoia and fear to bolster strength to ride out a storm of moral change while saying nothing?

In his 1947 classic *The Uneasy Conscience of Modern Fundamentalism*, Carl F. H. Henry called for "contemporary evangelicalism to reawaken to the relevance of its redemptive message to the global predicament." He believed that the truth was stronger than fiction and that evangelicals had a message for the world. He said, "The message for a decadent modern civilization must ring with the present tense. We must confront the world now with an ethics to make it tremble, and with a dynamic to give it hope."[15] So, if in any sense, we have shirked from this kind of optimism, Henry would no doubt be disappointed.

The "uneasy conscience" of which Henry spoke was the tendency of 1940s fundamentalists to grow uneasy with how to interact with a changing culture and retreat instead of engage. The fundamentalists were not uneasy about the truths of the Bible but rather with how to apply them well to the modern situation. I think for the growing evangelical minority today, the same temptation is present and, not knowing how to withstand the cultural pressures, the easiest thing to do appears to be to worry and retreat. But as Henry said, this mentality leaves no voice "speaking today as Paul would, either at the United Nations sessions, or at labor-management disputes, or in strategic university classrooms whether in Japan or Germany or America."[16] So there is a great need today for instructing evangelicals in how to engage the culture. In short, how then should the Christian live?

"Keep Calm and Carry On" Is Not the Gospel for Life

The idea of hunkering down in the face of shifting morality is something Martyn Lloyd-Jones likened to the Stoicism referenced in Acts 17. Lloyd-Jones, the medical doctor turned preacher, explained that in ancient times,

> The Stoic was a serious and thoughtful man, an honest one who believed in facing the facts of life. Having done so he had come to the conclusion that life is a difficult business and a hard task, and that there is only one way of going through with it and that is that you must exercise firm discipline upon yourself. Life, said the Stoic, will come and attack you, it will batter and beat you, and the great art of living, he said, is to remain standing on your feet.

And the only way to do it is to brace back your shoulders, to set a firm upper lip, to go in for the philosophy of courage, and say, "I am going to be a man!" . . . You just decide that you are not going to give in, you are not going to be defeated; whatever may happen to you, you are still standing, you are going on and you will stick it to the end. The philosophy of grit, the philosophy of courage, the philosophy of the stiff upper lip.[17]

This kind of Stoicism that is high on morality, asceticism, and indifference plays well in our day of mutual challenges to "just grind it out" to such a degree that there is a version of it we might call Evangelical Stoicism. Here, we self-philosophize when we counsel to "remind yourself at all times what you can control and what you can't." Evangelical Stoicism is a philosophy of coping that says, "We cannot control the weather or the economy, but we can control our thoughts and actions." From dieting, to keeping up with technology, to pursuing academic studies, to dealing with trials, to enduring family gatherings or tensions, we easily drift into Stoicism whether we know it or not.

We are quick to medicate, conflict-avoid, exaggerate, miscommunicate, deflect, blame, and hide. We minimize public embarrassment, overcompensate for errors, redouble our efforts, and study how better to manage our public profile. We are experts at "toughing it out." We read leadership and self-help books about how to succeed, how to press farther. We have gotten very good at being proficient, and we know how to get by.

In the face of the decline of cultural morality or in the wake of the redefinition of marriage, we hunker down and huddle up. Yet, simple joy, faith, hope, or thankfulness are missing as we "Keep Calm and Carry On."

This is not to say there isn't any value in perseverance or endurance. Indeed, in the Christian life, these are important stabilizers for living in the Spirit. But, often we live as if we are to do much on our own strength. When we pray or talk of prayer, we feel shame for what we perceive is a lack, a deficiency, a flaw. When we talk about the gospel, we don't think joyful thoughts, we feel guilt for something we haven't done or at a loss for something we really are not sure related to the present cultural debates. So we double down and try again. But doing these things apart from the Spirit isn't the gospel way. This is not what Christ meant for us when He said His burden was light.

How, then, are we to endure suffering that may come as a result of holding fast to biblical truth? How do you thrive in the workplace, in conversations with coworkers or at the family dinner table, or in the public square? What is more, how should Christians prepare to live and suffer for truth in a world where the standards of truth have changed? While now some may regularly endure hardship for the gospel, few of us are facing regular persecution. But how do we prepare for that day should it come?

For prison cells, tough callings, ridicule, persecution, or days worse than we can imagine?

Well, the Evangelical Stoicism on which we often stand just will not do. It is not the gospel way. As Lloyd-Jones said of Stoicism, "It may be very noble, I will grant you that, but it is noble paganism."[18]

In short, "Keep Calm and Carry On" is not the gospel for life. The better way is rooted in something far deeper and supernatural than what is found in our shallow pockets of grit and determination. The apostle Paul shows us how to live in what he recorded in his second letter to his disciple, Timothy.

A Letter from Prison

Paul's second letter to Timothy in the Bible is believed to be Paul's last. While personalized to Timothy and his work in Ephesus, clearly the teaching of the letter was intended for more readers. At the time of his writing, Paul was in prison likely facing execution, and because of this, as Calvin notes, "all that we read here . . . ought to be viewed by us as written not with ink but with Paul's own blood" for what he was suffering and sacrificing.[19]

Timothy was losing heart, undergoing difficulty, troubled at Paul's arrest, and in need of encouragement. The temptation toward enduring by stoic hand-wringing must have been strong.

Paul, however, was not losing any hope at all, for Paul was no Stoic.

What, then, is Paul's counsel and remedy for Timothy? How should Timothy prepare to endure the coming suffering and the change of the world around him? Paul gives gospel-centered advice in 2 Timothy 1:8–12 by way of a personal plea and the sharing of his conviction.

> Therefore do not be ashamed of the testimony about our Lord, nor of me his prisoner, but share in suffering for the gospel by the power of God, who saved us and called us to a holy calling, not because of our works but because of his own purpose and grace, which he gave us in Christ Jesus before the ages began, and which now has been manifested through the appearing of our Savior Christ Jesus, who abolished death and brought life and immortality to light through the gospel, for which I was appointed a preacher and apostle and teacher, which is why I suffer as I do. But I am not ashamed, for I know whom I have believed, and I am convinced that he is able to guard until that Day what has been entrusted to me.

If you were in prison and facing death, what would your final written letter contain? As 2 Timothy marks the last words of Paul written from death row, he is using his final letter to strengthen and provide hope for others. Specifically, in the case of Timothy, he is pleading with him.

Do Not Be Ashamed

From his reminder in 2 Timothy 1:7 that God did not give Timothy a "spirit of fear" to the command in 1:8 for Timothy not to be "ashamed of the testimony about our Lord, nor of me his prisoner," we get the picture that Timothy has lost his focus to some degree. Like Peter who, after seeing the wind while walking on the water toward Jesus, began to sink (Matt. 14:30), so Timothy seems to be sinking. When Paul uses the word "ashamed," it could be that he has in mind the words of Jesus in Mark 8:38: "For whoever is ashamed of me and my words in this adulterous and sinful generation, of him will the Son of Man also be ashamed."[20] Therefore, he pleads with Timothy not to be ashamed of two primary things.

First, Timothy should not be ashamed of "the testimony about our Lord." Very simply, Paul is saying, "Timothy, regardless of what comes, what happens to me, whatever the authorities do to you or the church, do not be ashamed of the gospel." What a wonderful definition of the gospel is found in this phrase, "the testimony about our Lord." Second, Timothy should not be ashamed of Paul while he is in prison. But note whose prisoner. Paul states he is the prisoner not of Rome, but of "our Lord."

Paul is in prison per the assignment and plans of Christ. Here Paul is reminding Timothy that no matter what happens in the world, Jesus Christ is still in control of all things and is holding all things together (Col. 1:17). This is no Stoic philosopher or the equivalent of a hunkered-down twenty-first-century American evangelical seeking to endure the inevitable. This is a confident, hope-filled Christian, clothed in the armor of God (Eph. 6).

Share in Suffering for the Gospel

Next, Paul pleads with Timothy to "share in suffering for the gospel." The pioneering New Testament scholar A. T. Robertson believed that Paul coined the Greek word behind this phrase to convey joint suffering for the gospel with both Jesus and Paul. By this, Paul reminds Timothy that whatever may come, he is not alone and is not the first to endure the pressures brought by a culture opposed to biblical truth. Further, in 1:16, Paul upholds the legacy of Onesiphorus as an example of this shared suffering. Onesiphorus, perhaps having died in this quest, was not ashamed of Paul or the gospel, and sought to find Paul "earnestly" so he could refresh him in his labors. This example is in contrast to the two others Paul mentions in 1:15 who were ashamed and who "turned away" from Paul. But the virtue here is not in which individual was stronger or was made of sterner stuff. Paul underscores in 1:8 that suffering done rightly is suffering done "by the power of God." That is, according to the power of God and the strength He provides. This is not suffering by grit. This is not Stoicism. Paul wanted Timothy to share in suffering that was beyond his strength so he could rely on God's power. Timothy was weakening, but God's power is made perfect in weakness (2 Cor. 12:9).

How do we share in suffering? How should the Christian live when faced with opposition to his stand for truth?

Practically, the advice of Paul here encourages the Christian to prepare now to suffer, to expect hardship and a culture of opposition to come, so when it arrives you will not be ashamed and not rely on your own Stoic attempts at self-reliance. Further, Paul's admonition encourages the Christian to stand with those who are already suffering.

In twenty-first-century American culture, the Christian should not sit idly by while his brothers and sisters in other states or cities are undergoing challenges for their articulation of what the Bible teaches about marriage. If our conviction is that God, through His Word, is clear on these matters, then we should not be ashamed to stand with those who believe the same and are now suffering for it. Yes, it may attract similar consequences for us, but that is not a reason for us to be ashamed or timid. Yet, as Paul states, such efforts to support like-minded believers should only be done by the power of God and in the Spirit of

Christ, which means speaking the truth, yes, but doing so in love (Eph. 4:15).

The core of Paul's plea to Timothy not to be ashamed and to share in suffering is the gospel. In short, Paul is saying to Timothy, "Right living in this world of opposition begins by remembering the gospel." Time spent recollecting the Good News is not a vain exercise for the Christian. In fact, it is exactly what the Evangelical Stoic needs. Paul's reminder of the gospel begins, in verse 9, with the phrase "who saved us and called us to a holy calling." The God who gives power to endure is first the God who saves and calls.

The notion of saving clearly communicates a rescue of eternal weight. Mark Dever helpfully teaches that salvation in the Bible can be thought of as past, present, and future. In the past, God saved us from the penalty of sin. In the present, God is saving us from the power of sin. In the future, God will save us from the presence of sin.[21] That God saves by a holy calling, too, is a reminder that in the wisdom of God, he has determined to give the second birth by calling people to it. Throughout the Bible, we see this functioning like two sides of the same coin, with the calling coming into the ears of hearers by the proclamation of the gospel from fellow humans. Whether on a train, around the dinner table, in a park, or a church service, God uses "someone preaching" (Rom. 10:14) to call them, while at the same time calling them by the work of the Holy Spirit (John 6:44; Titus 3:5).

The Gift of the Gospel Is Grace

Next, Paul states that this salvation from God is "not because of our works, but because of his own purpose and grace" (2 Tim. 1:9). The gift of the gospel rests in God's grace so that no one can boast of their own achievement of it (Eph. 2:8–9). This component alone undercuts the idea that we could ever "Keep Calm and Carry On" our way on earth to heaven. Rather, the emphasis of Paul's plea centers on "God's gracious purpose" in salvation.

God's ways are not ours. He purposes as He pleases, but He is good and so are His purposes. When we talk of God's working in salvation, often great angst ensues—but this need not be the case. Overall, we should affirm that it is a good thing that God is the author of salvation, for when we pray for God to work in the heart of our neighbor, God can and will. Thus, God's purpose and grace in salvation should be a joyful thing to affirm and even sing. For Timothy, it should have served as a reminder of God's grace to him and also to Paul.

This is not the issuing of the Stoic-prescribed, "Think about only what you can control" mantra. Rather it is, even if we do not understand it, "Remember God is in control!" This is helpfully portrayed in William Cowper's "God Moves in a Mysterious Way."

God moves in a mysterious way
His wonders to perform;
He plants his footsteps in the sea
And rides upon the storm.

Judge not the Lord by feeble sense,
But trust him for his grace;
Behind a frowning providence
He hides a smiling face.

Deep in unfathomable mines
Of never-failing skill,
He treasures up his bright designs
And works his sov'reign will.

His purposes will ripen fast,
Unfolding ev'ry hour;
The bud may have a bitter taste,
But sweet will be the flow'r.

Ye fearful saints, fresh courage take;
The clouds ye so much dread
Are big with mercy, and shall break
In blessings on your head.

Blind unbelief is sure to err
And scan His work in vain;
God is his own interpreter,
And he will make it plain.[22]

Paul continues to remind that this grace is the thing God "gave us in Christ Jesus before the ages began." Grace is the gift given in God's saving us and it was given in Jesus. Salvation is rooted always in God the Son, for no saving is possible apart from him (Acts 4:12). Yet, this gift was given long before we or Paul or Timothy were born and before they did any works.

Grace was given "before the ages began" and thus is not a new idea or a Plan B recovery idea. Salvation has been in God's mind since before time and was brought about on his timetable. Because of this we can have confidence that he will bring it to completion on his timetable as well (Phil. 1:6). Thus, in 2 Timothy 1:10, Paul continues to explain that God's gift of grace "now has been manifested" in the present and here we see, again, that salvation is both beyond time and in time. It is both timeless and timely. Like the conclusion of a long novel, in Colossians 1:26 Paul refers to this work of God as a mystery now revealed. The revelation of salvation came through "our Savior Christ Jesus." His appearing as the incarnated God-man truly is the epicenter of all of history. The Old Testament faithful looked forward to that day and were saved by grace through their faith. All who came and come after look back to that day and are also saved by grace. Just like the majority of believers throughout the centuries, though we have never seen Him with our eyes we love Him and believe in Him, and the result, Peter says, is "the salvation of our souls" (1 Pet. 1:8–9).

The Work of Christ in Three Phrases

At this point in his letter, to underscore the importance of his plea for Timothy to remember the gospel, he uses three vital phrases to describe the magnitude of the work of Christ. First, he says Jesus "abolished death." This is the same phrase he uses in 1 Corinthians 15:26, "The last enemy to be destroyed is death," and in Hebrews 2:14–15 when he talks of Jesus destroying "the one who has the power of death." Just as was prophesied in

Genesis 3:15, through His death and resurrection, Jesus Christ crushes the Serpent, Satan, and brings about the death of death.

Second, Paul states that Jesus "brought to light" life and immortality. The idea he conveys here is that of turning on the lights like in 1 Corinthians 4:5 where light is brought to things "now hidden in darkness," and in Ephesians 1:18 where salvation is described as the enlightenment of the eyes of one's heart. Bringing to light life and immortality is another way of saying unchangeable or immortal life. In contrast to the defeated death of death, Jesus brings light of immortal life. From God speaking into the darkness in Genesis 1 to the Lord God serving as the only light reigning forever in Revelation 22, light is used throughout the Bible to show transformed newness.

How these works of eternal weight and infinite size are brought to the likes of Timothy and to us, Paul explains in his third phrase, "through the gospel." Through the gospel, death died and life was lit. Through the gospel, or as we saw earlier the "testimony of the Lord Jesus," man was gloriously reconciled to God. For Timothy, regardless of fears, failures, threats, and pressures, this miraculous Good News is worth resting in and singing about.

Remember the Gospel

The Stoic and his self-reliance cannot rejoice in this and will not, but the Christian can and should. In verse 11 and the start of verse 12 Paul concludes his plea by telling Timothy that this gospel is the reason why he is where he is, and is why he has done what he has done. The message of the powerful and life-changing work of Christ is what Paul has been appointed to proclaim as God's messenger. Finally, he reminds, the only thing for which he is guilty is faithfulness to the gospel.

In light of Timothy's fears and apprehensions in facing opposition and coming conflict, Paul first pleads with Timothy to remember the gospel. For the Evangelical Stoic, this might seem a bit basic. "I have the gospel; what I need is what to do next?" And yet, that thinking only reveals that the Evangelical Stoic is well on his way down the wrong path. Golf is a sport that requires a great deal of practice and regular play to enjoy and perform well. But, as often happens, if much effort is extended but in bad habits or a poor swing, you will just be very good at being a poor golfer. For the Evangelical Stoic who opts to move beyond the gospel ABCs and onto other "practical matters" of how best to "grind it out" and endure, he is one who has just become very good at getting off track and into a rut.

Paul's admonition to remember the gospel is one that defeats self-reliance, stoicism, and many other "isms." The gospel should remind us, moment by moment, that we are in need of grace and that we cannot do anything apart from Christ. It should drive us to prayer and daily fellowship with God. It should humble us when in an argument. It should cause us to serve others rather than seek to be served. It should drive us to fight temptation, flee sin, proclaim hope, and to seek joy. In short, reminding oneself of the gospel is one of the most practical things one can do.

God Is Able

When thinking further about how the Christian should live in our world of rapid social change, we are helped by Paul's second statement of advice to Timothy. After pleading with him, Paul now shares his conviction that serves as another foundation for his endurance and joy regardless of the circumstances. Paul begins verse 12 with a statement referencing back to 1:8 when he says essentially to Timothy, "I told you not to be ashamed of the gospel because I am not ashamed."

Even though he is in prison for faithfulness to the gospel, he is not ashamed of the gospel. He begins his explanation with the contrasting word, "But"—and in just those three letters there lies an ocean filled with the fruit of the Spirit. In essence, Paul is saying, "Even though I suffer, even though I am in prison unjustly, even though many have abandoned me, even though this was not my plan . . . but I am not ashamed."

In this one word, there exists enough joy to fill a jail cell. This one word is broad enough and strong enough on which to build a house of faith and a life of trust. For with this word, Paul is showing how he is, in the words of 1 Peter 4:19, "entrusting his soul to a faithful Creator." No matter what change comes, or what standards of truth fall, Paul is not wringing his hands nor attempting to stir up his own internal strength. For as Paul states, "For I know whom I have believed, and I am convinced" (2 Tim. 1:12).

Paul knows Jesus Christ (Phil. 3:10). He believes in Him and trusts Him and this is the model for how the Christian should live. In times of testing and opposition, what you know is important, but even the Evangelical Stoic knows much. More than what is known is Who is known. Do you know Jesus Christ?

We meet Him in his Word and there we are reminded that He is good. He does not lie and He is gracious to His children. In His Word we find truth and strength to resist temptation and fight the evil one. Even when we feel like we are going to break in two, when we come to His Word, we are reminded by Him that "a bruised reed he will not break, and a smoldering wick he will not quench" (Matt. 12:20), and that even if you "are so utterly burdened beyond [your] strength" and despair of life itself, that is to make you rely not on yourself "but on God who raises the dead" (2 Cor. 1:8–9).

The core of Paul's conviction is that God is able. In addi-
tion to remembering the gospel, there is this further source of
related strength that God is able that is diametrically opposite
the Evangelical Stoicism and the philosophy of "toughing it out."
For Paul knows what the Bible affirms over and over again, that
we are not able. We are finite creatures, weighed down with
the fragilities brought by sin, staring straight into the truth of
Jesus' words in John 15:5, "Apart from me you can do nothing."
Likewise, the Bible affirms that God is able. For example, when
Daniel's three friends refused to worship Nebuchadnezzar's gods
and were threatened by him with the furnace of fire, they said,
"If this be so, our God whom we serve is able to deliver us from
the burning fiery furnace, and he will deliver us out of your
hand, O king. But if not, be it known to you, O king, that we
will not serve your gods or worship the golden image that you
have set up" (Dan. 3:17–18). The God of the Bible is the God
who is able "to do far more abundantly than all we ask or think
(Eph. 3:20).

Specifically, Paul is convinced that God is able "to guard
until that Day what has been entrusted to me" (2 Tim. 1:12).
Here he is telling Timothy that the reason he can rejoice and
endure is because he knows God is able to protect the most
important thing, his eternal life. When Paul uses the words
guard and *entrusted*, he conveys the idea of protecting his deposit
against robbery. We know from verse 9 that deposit is namely the

gospel of grace given to Paul; that is, his salvation. Paul is certain that God is able to protect his salvation "until that Day" or the day of Jesus' return. God secured all of this before time began, and thus will guard it until time ends. Thus, all other matters are temporary in comparison.

What if you could see into the future and know all the outcomes of your circumstances? Would it change your perspective on any present sufferings? Would it change how you endured if you knew how everything was going to turn out?

Paul has seen into the future, and has conviction that is sure. He is convinced God is able. Through the reading of God's Word with the help of the Holy Spirit, we can have the same conviction of hope as Paul. Regardless of the changing moral landscape, the Christian should live with the perspective of rest and contentment in the fact that God is able.

The Gospel for Life

With regard to the cultural institutionalization of same-sex marriage, how should the Christian live? How should the Christian relate to neighbors living in a same-sex marriage? How should the Christian respond in a corporate environment that affirms same-sex marriage? How should the Christian weather the increasingly dominant media and pop-culture atmosphere that affirms same-sex marriage?

While the specific steps forward in response to these questions might be varied or driven by context, overall the Christian has a choice to engage or retreat. The temptation to retreat either in word or in indifference will come. Here Paul's counsel to Timothy not to be ashamed should ring loud and fan in to flame courage. But even for those who nobly stand, even here the temptation will come toward Evangelical Stoicism, with hand-wringing and digging in, seeking to endure in a "Keep Calm and Carry On" fashion. But, as we have seen, this too, is not the gospel way. For even though the Evangelical Stoic may stand for gospel truth, standing for any issue in state self-reliance is a form of gospel abandonment.

In the last quarter of his life, Carl F. H. Henry observed that, "The evangelical movement looks stronger than in fact it is. . . . But no earthly movement holds the Lion of the Tribe of Judah by the tail. We may need for a season to be encaged in the Lion's den until we recover an apostolic awe of the Risen Christ, the invincible Head of a dependent body sustained by his supernatural power. Apart from life in and by the Spirit we are all pseudo-evangelicals."[23]

Indeed, instead of "The Uneasy Conscience of Modern Fundamentalism" in Henry's day, we wrestle with "The Self-Reliant Conscience of Evangelical Stoicism." Yet, as Paul pleads and reminds, the way to live in a sea of social change is to remember the gospel, that God is able. As the P. P. Bliss hymn says,

When peace like a river attendeth my way,
When sorrows like sea billows roll,
Whatever my lot, thou has taught me to say,
It is well, it is well, with my soul![24]

For the sporting arena or wartime morale, the Stoicism of "Keep Calm and Carry On" may be a fitting remedy for winning. But for the advance of the gospel in our hearts, in times of suffering in prison cells around the world, or for just working through how to respond well to changing social standards at home, the "It Is Well, He Is Able" approach might be more revolutionary for instructing Christians on how they should live.

"It Is Well, He Is Able" is the *gospel for life*.

Discussion Questions

1. If you were in prison and facing death, what would your final written letter contain?
2. Do you find yourself anxious about the cultural changes in our present day?
3. What difficulties will Christians experience in culture as the result of same-sex marriage becoming institutionalized?

4

How Should the Church Engage?

J. D. Greear

OUR CULTURE PUTS FORWARD THE NARRATIVE THAT WE really only have two options in our relationship with the LGBT community—affirmation or alienation. Jesus shows us that a third response—a *gospel* response—is possible. He shows us how to respond with grace and truth, how to hold out God's truth *and* God's love, not having to choose between the two.

Jesus' ministry was a paradox. Never was there anyone who exalted God's standards of righteousness so consistently. He said that He did not come to abolish *any* part of the law, that if our righteousness did not exceed the righteousness of the Pharisees and the Sadducees, we would never even see the kingdom of God. But at the same time, never was there anyone who so effectively gathered the outcasts. The oppressed and the oppressors both sat at His feet. The religious people of His day could not understand Him. How could someone on intimate terms with God be so attractive to sinful people? The secular powers hated Him because He presented a challenge to their absolute claims to authority. The last week of Jesus' life captures this paradox perfectly. His crucifixion was a joint project of both religious and secular power, while a former prostitute washed His feet with her tears and a thief defended His reputation from the cross.

The apostle John captured the heart of Jesus' ministry in John 1:14 when he described Jesus as a man "full of grace and truth." Truth without grace is fundamentalism; grace without truth is sentimentality. Compromising either one for the sake of the other makes us unlike Jesus. So to represent Jesus to the LGBT community, we want to be full of both. And when we are full of grace and truth like Jesus, we can expect to see the response he did—to repel the proud and attract the broken.

Jesus' preaching in the Gospels gives us ways that we can model such a ministry of grace and truth. While we will often fail to represent Christ perfectly, this represents what every church should aspire to be.

We Will Be Friends of the LGBT Community

Jesus presents the way we should engage the LGBT community in one of the most misinterpreted things He ever said: "Judge not, that you be not judged" (Matt. 7:1). This is an incredibly popular verse in today's culture, but most people take it to mean something Jesus never intended. People bandy about "judge not" as if Jesus was advocating pluralism, making sure that we never tell anyone that what they're doing is wrong. But Jesus couldn't have meant that.

Just a few verses later, Jesus says, "The gate is wide and the way is easy that leads to destruction, and those who enter by it are many. For the gate is narrow and the way is hard that leads to life, and those who find it are few" (Matt. 7:13–14). In fact, here's how Jesus characterized His whole life: "[The world] hates me because I testify about it that its works are evil" (John 7:7). That's not a guy walking around in Birkenstocks, saying, "It's okay, man. Who am I to judge? I mean, it's legal now in Colorado."

Jesus' followers followed the same pattern. Paul commanded Christians in Ephesians to *rebuke* the works of darkness. John the Baptist *confronted* Herod and his wife on their policy of open marriage—and lost his head for it. Did Jesus respond by saying that John should have just kept his opinion to himself? No, Jesus called John the Baptist the greatest man ever born. So "judge not" cannot mean that we don't tell our community when God's

Word says something is wrong. That's simply not what Jesus meant.

Judgment, according to Jesus, isn't declaring a certain controversial truth. It's what you do *after* you tell someone the truth that determines if you are judging them. As Jesus said, "God did not send his Son into the world to condemn [or judge] the world, but in order that the world might be saved through him" (John 3:17). Even though Jesus told many people that their works were evil, He still did not condemn that world. How could that be? Because after telling us the truth, *Jesus brought us close.* He made sinners—you and me—His friends. You judge someone not when you assess their position, but when you dismiss them as a person.

Have you drawn the gay and lesbian community close? Are you their friend? Will gay and lesbian people feel welcome in your home? When you meet someone who is gay, do you see him or her—first and foremost—as a person created in the image of God? Are you among the chief advocates against abuse, injustice, and discrimination against the gay and lesbian community in our society? When Jesus died on a cross, He didn't die for heterosexuals. He died for *every* human being, which means that His love extends to every human being.

As believers, we have to love our gay neighbor more than we love our position on sexual morality. Our relationship with them must not be contingent upon their agreeing with us about sexuality. We should never compromise our position or fail to state it, but even when others disagree with it, we do not cut them off; we draw them close.

We Will Not Stigmatize or Single Out Sexual Sin

Stigmatizing sexual sin shows extreme ignorance of the gospel. Look at what Jesus says in Matthew 7:2–5:

> "For with the judgment you pronounce you will
> be judged, and with the measure you use it will be
> measured to you. Why do you see the speck that is in
> your brother's eye, but do not notice the log that is in
> your own eye? Or how can you say to your brother,
> 'Let me take the speck out of your eye,' when there is
> the log in your own eye? You hypocrite, first take the
> log out of your own eye, and then you will see clearly
> to take the speck out of your brother's eye."

Many think that Jesus is addressing direct hypocrisy here (and He is), but the bigger problem He's pointing to is our failure to grapple with our own inherent sinfulness. Jesus *assumes* that the log is in our eye. Christian doctrine teaches that every human heart is deeply depraved, like a polluted well. Without Christ, what flows out of every one of our hearts is not pure. And when we act like one brand of sin is particularly heinous, it only proves that we haven't fully grappled with the pollution in our own hearts.

My first dorm in college had well water. It was near a lake and the water that would come out of the spigot tasted like fish. Not pleasant. My roommate and I tried to cover it up by making lemonade out of the water. We had to add so much sugar to cover up the fish taste that the result was the consistency of maple syrup. It was one of those solutions that only college freshmen would think up. Because, of course, we really didn't take out the fish taste. We just covered it up with other things. Whatever mildly poisonous fishiness was in the water . . . well, we still drank it. That's the kind of image Jesus uses for the human heart. Religion doesn't take away our heart's pollution. It simply covers it up. As John Owen once said, "The seed of every sin is in every human heart." Those who recognize that truth about themselves speak with a deep humility, with a palpable brokenness. We are sinners, one and all, and whenever we talk about "sin," we need to do so as Paul did, reminding ourselves that "Christ Jesus came into the world to save sinners, of whom I am the foremost" (1 Tim. 1:15).

Jesus illustrated this perfectly in His parable of a man who owed his master "10,000 talents." A talent was an enormous unit of money, so much so that to say "10,000 talents" was like us saying, "a bazillion dollars." It was, for all intents and purposes, an infinite debt. But when the due date comes, this man shows up in court, falls on his knees, and pleads for mercy: "Sir, please give me just a little bit more time."

In those days, if you couldn't pay your debts, you or your children would go to prison, becoming slaves until the debt was absolved. This could take generations, and with a debt of 10,000 talents, the future must have looked grim. But his request is pitiful. "Please, just give me another week." It's a ridiculous request, really. Another week—honestly, another ten thousand weeks— would not give him the ability to pay back this debt. He's sunk, but here he is blubbering and making this pathetic spectacle to his lender. Everyone watching is getting embarrassed, because, of course, lenders aren't known for their mercy. We call them loan *sharks*, after all, not loan *puppies*.

But the most unexpected thing happens. This loan shark gets a tear in his eye, and he feels an emotion that Jesus calls *splagma*, a gut-level compassion. He looks the man in the eye and says, "Stand up. You don't have another week to pay me back . . . because you don't owe me any more money at all. As of this moment, your debt is resolved in the presence of all of these witnesses, and you are forgiven." The man can't understand it. He feels as light as air and walks out of the courtroom, giddy with excitement.

But then he spots his friend across the street, a guy who owes him a dollar fifty for a Mountain Dew. He says to his friend, "Hey, give me my dollar fifty!" But when the man asks for a little more time, he replies, "No! If you don't give me my money *now*, then you are going to prison."

It's at this point in the story when everyone listening to Jesus would have stopped Him. "What? There is *no way* somebody would act like that after being forgiven so much." To which Jesus says: "*Exactly.*" If you are characterized by disgust over someone else's sin rather than being overwhelmed at the forgiveness that God has given you, you are desperately out of touch with the gospel.

We Will Preach God's Design for Sexuality, Not Merely Its Aberrations

Those who wish to justify the gay lifestyle claim that Jesus never talked about homosexuality. This is a claim that is true only in the most technical and unhelpful sense. No, Jesus never uttered the word *homosexual*, but he also never mentioned rape, child abuse, fraud, or idolatry. But his stance on each of those issues is, nevertheless, quite clear.

There are two ways that Jesus could have established what was right and wrong in regards to sexuality. He could have talked about every possible variation of the wrong, condemning each aberration one by one. Or He could put forward a vision for what is right. Think of it like this: if five women were standing side by side, and one of them was my wife, I could identify her in two ways: I could say that each of the other four were *not* my wife; or I could say, "That wonderful woman there . . . *she's* my wife." Jesus repeatedly affirmed the Mosaic understanding of the sanctity of sex within heterosexual marriage, and by doing that He disallowed all deviations.

We have to follow Jesus' example, putting forward a positive vision for sexuality. According to the apostle Paul in 1 Corinthians 6, the biblical view of sex is the loftiest view imaginable. Sex is a profound union between two independent beings, a physical union that should be accompanied by union and oneness in every other area. This is why sex outside of a marital context is so damaging. Anything less than a complete and total unity in the covenant relationship of marriage is subhuman.

God's design for sex, however, was intended to be a tangible representation of an entire relationship. It is meant to reflect a unity between two genders that are other, an image of God's love for the *other*—us. Sex is not merely a physical activity, but a reflection of our Creator. We need to recover that side of sexuality, preaching the positive and beautiful dimensions of covenant love and sex. Christians of all people should not be afraid of sex. God designed it and He delights in it. We must recover some of that delight.

We Will Begin with a Call to Repentance

According to the gospel of Mark, the first word out of Jesus' mouth as He announced His Kingdom was "repent." In our day, that word brings up images of angry preachers with sandwich boards. But repentance simply means that we acknowledge Jesus' lordship instead of our own. Every generation inevitably establishes a standard for what is right and wrong. We're all moral. The gay community is intensely moral. But the worst condemnation given in the Bible is that a certain generation did what was right *in their own eyes.* "They did what was right," means a group of people was morally conscious, even morally fervent. But "in their own eyes" means their own sensibilities were the standard. Coming to Jesus means we stop using our hearts as the beginning point for determining what is right and wrong, submitting instead to His Word. This is painful for all of us.

The Bible is an equal opportunity offender, but the specific aspect of Jesus' lordship that offends people will vary from generation to generation. In one generation, it is teachings against militarism and violence, in another it is the equality and dignity of all peoples, in another it is His design for sexuality. I cannot judge the hearts of those Christians who affirm the gay lifestyle, but I can point out that the shift in their thinking appears to be part of a larger bending to the culture. They seem to find a new way to read the Bible in order to justify what the culture sees as right in its own eyes, despite the fact that for two thousand years, Christians have understood this to be a clear issue. We're coming to a point when we've got to choose whether we are going to have the disapproval of the world or the disapproval of Jesus.

We Will Not Be Bullied into Silence

We commonly hear that by teaching about the sin of same-sex behavior, we are propagating hate speech. I've received packages—more than once—at my house, telling me that I am responsible for the suicides of gay people. This grieves me deeply: it pains me when gay or lesbian people take their lives. But if the biblical view of sexuality is true, how can it be loving to *not* tell them? If the biblical view is true, it would actually be hateful—or at least severely delinquent cowardice—not to tell them.

People often ask me, "What if *your* son declares one day that he is gay?" If I love him (and I do!), I will tell him what God's Word says plainly. If I refuse to do that, I'm not loving him; I'm implicitly condemning him. And I hope I can teach him, like his daddy, to come to the feet of Jesus, broken and repentant—repentant for the wickedness in our hearts that neither of us have a way of excising. If he was born with a proclivity toward same-sex behavior and I was born with a proclivity toward anger, pride, deceit, and unfaithfulness—well, we *both* need to be born again. After all, no one goes to hell for being homosexual. How do I know that? Because no one goes to heaven for being hetero-sexual. The only choice that puts a person outside of God's grace is refusing to acknowledge their brokenness and submit to Jesus' lordship.

And what if my son and I come to a point where we don't agree about this issue? Then I will seek to do what Jesus did. I won't judge him or send him away. I will keep bringing him close, but I will warn him that the Bible says a day of judgment is coming. When we push someone away after speaking truth, we have judged them and failed to represent our Savior; but when we say, "Peace!" and there is no peace, we have failed in our respon-sibility as watchmen on the walls.

Sexual Passions Can Change, Though It May Not Happen in This Life

Richard Hays of Duke University, in his book *Moral Vision of the New Testament*, says that the already-not-yet dimension of the Kingdom provides the answer to whether gays and lesbians should expect to change their sexual passions upon coming to Christ. Already-not-yet means that Jesus has inaugurated His Kingdom and we *already* experience certain elements of His power, but much of Jesus' ultimate healing works have *not yet* come. Physical healing works like this. Sometimes Jesus will heal as a sign of the Kingdom, but sometimes we have to wait for the resurrection for ultimate healing. In other words, many godly people still die of cancer. It's not because they don't have faith; it's because their ultimate healing comes in the resurrection. I can look in my own heart and see sins from which Jesus has healed me. I am in many ways a changed man, but I still yearn for redemption and healing from other things. None of us will be made completely whole until Christ returns.

In the same way, we preach the already-not-yet of the Kingdom in regards to sexuality. I know of people who have seen God work dramatically in the area of their sexual desires. But for others, God allows people to struggle so that they can be a testimony to God's sustaining grace *in struggle*. It seems that the latter is actually God's normal way. John Newton, the writer of "Amazing Grace," came to this realization late in his life, after getting frustrated by seeing the same sins attack him in his eighties that had plagued him in his twenties. He came to see that God allows us to continue struggling with indwelling sin to convince us—until our dying breath—of our desperate need for grace. Christian growth this side of heaven is not getting to a point where you don't feel like you need grace anymore (which is how most of us think of Christian growth). Christian growth is becoming more intimately aware of how desperately we need grace.

I recently received a letter from a guy in our church, telling me about his journey with same-sex attraction. He wrote:

You recently preached a sermon in which you clearly laid out the gospel—that Jesus had taken away *all* of my guilt and shame by bearing it Himself, that I was not just forgiven, but was made pure by the blood of Christ.

And at that moment, it all began to make sense. My same-sex desires do not define me. My identity is built on something so much greater: the resurrected savior Jesus Christ. God knew me from before the foundation of the world, He knew my sin, He knew my struggles, and He still chose to send His Son to live the perfect life I could never live and die the death that I deserved. On the cross, He traded places with me, taking my sin and shame and giving me His place of righteousness with the Father. I am in Christ. I am a new creation.

When I saw this, I began to see my struggle with same-sex attraction as a way for me to draw closer to Christ, as a way for me to see my own sinfulness and be driven even more to treasure the gospel, to treasure the fact that in Christ I am fully known and fully loved. And eternity became so much sweeter knowing that even if I struggle in this world for the rest of my life, one day I will be with my Savior and be completely freed from this body of sin forever.

Is it possible for God to change our sexual passions? Over time, and with great struggle, yes. But God doesn't change us immediately or magically, and for most of us, what we struggle with today will continue to be a struggle until Christ returns. What we must remember is that whatever defined us *before* coming to Christ no longer defines us *in* Christ. And one day, by His grace, we will be made whole.

We Will Present the Multifaceted Beauty of the Gospel

Whenever Jesus dealt with someone in sexual sin, He never started with the sin. He always started with the root issues behind the sin. In the gospel of John, for instance, He deals with two different women caught in sexual sin. In John 4, He meets a woman who is a serial adulterer. She has had five husbands and the man she shacks up with now is not her husband. But He doesn't just say, "Stop it!" He shows her that her addictive behavior is driven by a soul thirst, and the water she was craving was not found in romance, but in knowing His everlasting love. The Savior gave her the perfect love she had always been looking for: He knew everything about her life and yet loved her entirely. This loving acceptance—not advice about how to change—was the water of life that delivered her from her captivity to sex.

But perhaps the clearest demonstration of this point is in John 8. A woman caught in the act of adultery is brought to Jesus, and what does He say? "Neither do I condemn you. Go and sin no more." I've always been amazed at the order in which He put those two statements. Most of us would have put change before acceptance: clean up your act and come back when you've gotten your life together. But Jesus knew she would never have the power to change until she had felt the weight of His acceptance. God's acceptance is the power that liberates us from sin. It is not the reward for us having liberated ourselves.

That means I don't just tell the girl who has lost her virginity about the dangers of venereal disease or the shamefulness of sleeping around. I tell her that there is a God who cared so much about her that He pursued her, left heaven to come and take upon Himself the shame of her sin so He could wash her and make her pure and holy in His sight. I tell her that the only way she will ever break the stronghold of idolatry is by seeing that there is a Father whose attention is better and whose love is more steadfast than the arms of any boy.

It means I don't just tell the young man struggling with pornography about how destructive his habit is. I tell him that there is a heavenly Father who has set him apart for His purpose, sacrificed Himself so that he could live free from sin as a valiant man of honor. I tell him that Jesus' last words on the cross were not, "Go fix yourself," but, "It is finished!"

Only the weightiness of God's acceptance can empower us to forsake idolatry. Our message is not simply, "Stop sexual sin." Our message is, "Behold your God!" Only amazement at the love of God for us can deliver us from all the lesser attractions.

We Will Not Fear Suffering

We won't be the first generation to suffer for faithfulness to the Christian confession. In fact, in many ways, we are one of the only ones in history who never really *has* suffered. My question, then, is a sobering one: Are we ready to suffer? Will we have the courage to lose our reputation, to have our congregations shrink, to go to prison for the sake of the gospel? Speaking with grace and truth will come at a cost, and we need to prepare ourselves to pay that price, come what may.

I can just imagine a "John the Baptist" situation happening in our day. John was beheaded because he publicly confronted Herod for sexual sin, which made Herod's stepdaughter feel bad. Had that happened today, the blogosphere would erupt. "John, if you had just kept to 'grace and love and healing,' you'd still be alive. What a waste, John!" But Jesus commended John for speaking the truth. The violent spirit of John the Baptist's executors is very much alive in our world today. Is the courageous spirit of John the Baptist alive in us?

The Gospel Is the Center of Our Message

In his *Mere Christianity*, C. S. Lewis has a chapter on sexual ethics, which he recognizes will strike many readers as offensive. So he concludes by saying (in essence), "Does the Bible's teaching on sexuality bother you? Can you not get around it? Well then, punt it for a while, because the center of Christianity isn't sexual ethics. The center of Christianity is the cross and the lordship of Jesus. Wrestle with *that*, and if you come to understand that Jesus is who He says He is, then let Him lead you in the areas of sexuality. Don't start with questions about sex; start with Jesus."

I know that the Bible's teaching on sexuality can be an enormous barrier for people, so I frequently ask seekers who come to our church to punt the issue. "Take time to figure out who Jesus is," I tell them. "If you conclude, as I have, that He is Lord, then trust Him and let Him lead you on this issue. Sexual ethics are not the center of Christianity, the gospel is. Sexual ethics should not be central or dominant in our message—His cross should be."

At the same time, we have to address the question when it is brought to us, just as John the Baptist did. We can't go on punting this issue forever. We can't let grace crowd out truth; we must speak both grace *and* truth. And the only guide for holding both together is the gospel. The cross of Jesus shows us how to respond in confusing and turbulent times—not by shying away, but by laying down our lives for the sake of others.

Conclusion

I am privileged to pastor in the Raleigh-Durham area of North Carolina. Every weekend, in our congregation, we have upwards of two thousand college students from UNC, NC State, Duke, and NC Central. As a pastor of so many students, I deal with issues of sexuality on a weekly basis. This is not a theological debate for me, not a political angle. I cannot think of these issues without thinking of some very dear friends. In short, every time I approach the issue of sexuality, I approach it *pastorally*.

I think, for instance, of Brennan, a young man in our church—and a close, personal friend. He was very active in our leadership for many years, but he had a secret. He had a same-sex attraction that had led to several bouts with pornography and a string of hook-ups with guys he met in chat rooms. He has wrestled with this now for several years.

Recently, Brennan and I had a long conversation. "You know," he said, "I understand that acting on this is wrong. I can't read the Bible in a responsible way and not conclude that. But there's no way I *chose* to be like this. It wasn't like in seventh grade I suddenly decided this is how I want to be. I was never abused or anything. It just seems to be something that I've always had with me even though in many ways I have it under control. I imagine that this is going to be a struggle for me, until the day that I die."

I remain very close to Brennan. I love him. My kids love him. I've had to learn not merely to answer Brennan's theological questions, but to feel his pain, to grapple with his questions from his point of view.

Or I think of Gina. I first met Gina in a cell phone store where she worked. Her coworker and I invited Gina to visit our church. Gina had never really been to church before. She was in her early thirties and had been a practicing lesbian since college. She also battled severe depression. Once, in the midst of her depression, she drove to the Blue Ridge Mountains, where she planned to take her own life. She was about thirty minutes from where she had planned to jump when she received a phone call. It was her coworker: "I don't know where you are," she said, "but I woke up this morning thinking about you. I felt like God put you on my heart. I just wanted to say that I love you."

Gina was floored. She explained what she had been planning, and this girl talked her out of it. Gina checked herself into a hospital. Eventually Gina became a believer, and she is now active in our church. She heads up many of our overseas mission efforts, particularly in South Asia. She still struggles with these issues, but is following hard after God. I love Gina. She is a friend of our family. Any discussion on topics of sexuality makes me think about her and what's happening in her life.

I also know that every time I talk about same-sex attraction, that there are many listening to me who have been hurt or ostracized over this issue. Parents have disowned kids who confessed same-sex attraction. That's simply heartbreaking: at the time when they needed the constant love of a parent most, they instead faced rejection. Even more tragically, this rejection is sometimes done in the name of Christ. What greater lie can we tell about our Savior than to distance ourselves from the hurting and broken in the moment they would need us most?

So if you want to preach like Jesus, plunge yourself deep into the gospel. Study it, not like a seminarian studies doctrine, not like a politician studies a poll or an apologist studies an argument, but like you would study a sunset that leaves you speechless. The more you know of God's great love for you, the more love will spill out of you toward others. The more we become aware of how far Jesus reached to save us, the more we will overflow with grace and compassion toward others. As John says, "We love because He first loved us" (1 John 4:19). The more we are saturated with His love, the more we love in response. And the more we believe the gospel, the more we become like the gospel—overflowing with grace.

Discussion Questions

1. Have you drawn the gay and lesbian community close? Are you their friend?

2. What are practical ways that we can demonstrate love to our LGBT neighbors?

3. How do Christians learn to live as an increasingly minority voice in today's culture?

5

What Does the Culture Say?

R. Albert Mohler Jr.

THE SEXUAL REVOLUTION PRESENTS AN ENORMOUS AND urgent challenge to the Christian church in the West. The church has, of course, faced enormous theological challenges in the past. These are not the first revolutionary times that have demanded a Christian response, nor will they be the last. At the same time, the sexual revolution poses unique challenges to the Christian church and demands careful biblical, theological, and cultural analysis. For example, as British theologian Theo Hobson noted, "Churches have always faced difficult moral issues and they have muddled through . . . but it becomes ever clearer that the issue of homosexuality really is different."[25] In other words, the sexual revolution challenges the very heart of Christian conviction and faithfulness.

Another aspect of this revolution, indeed one of the most daunting aspects, is what Hobson calls "the sheer speed of the homosexual cause's success." As he describes it: "Something that was assumed for centuries to be unspeakably immoral has emerged as an alternative form of life, an identity that merits legal protection. The demand for gay equality has basically ousted traditionalist sexual morality from the moral high ground."[26] That is a profoundly important point. Hobson is arguing that this revolution, unlike any other, has actually turned the tables on Christianity in Western civilization.

Consider how this happened even in the last few decades. In the United States, evangelicals have enjoyed social and cultural status. We have had access to arenas of influence and we have been accustomed to social respect and credibility. The sexual revolution has changed all of that. Now in the eyes of the secular world, Christians—and evangelicals in particular—are considered to be an embarrassment. The new moral regime demands we surrender historic Christian conviction to the new sexual anarchy. But faithfulness to Christ and theological integrity demands that we continue with fidelity to the faith once for all delivered to the saints and stand with the historic Christian church and the authority of Scripture.

The New Intellectual Climate

The new sexual morality did not emerge from a vacuum. Massive intellectual changes at the worldview level over the last two hundred years set the stage for the revolution in which we currently find ourselves. We are living in times rightly, if rather awkwardly, described as the "late modern age." Modernity has brought many cultural goods, but it has also, as predicted, brought a radical change in the way citizens of Western societies think, feel, relate, and reason. The Enlightenment's liberation of reason at the expense of revelation was followed by a radical anti-supernaturalism that can scarcely be exaggerated. Looking at Europe and Great Britain, it is clear that the modern age has alienated an entire civilization from its Christian roots, along with Christian moral and intellectual commitments.

Furthermore, all this has to be put into the larger context of changes that have transformed the way most people in Western societies *think*. The moral revolution is part of the larger picture of a seismic shift in Western culture that has occurred over the last two centuries. In that span of time vast social changes have transformed the way people in advanced industrialized economies live, relate, and engage the larger world. If that sounds like an overstatement, just consider the fact that at the beginning of the twentieth century most Americans lived in a rural context as part of an extended family and with a range of geographic mobility that was generally confined to a very small area. The idea that human beings would be flung coast to coast in an advanced economy and that work would be transformed from the tilling of the soil to what is now described as "knowledge work" is something that would have been inconceivable.

These cultural transformations have uniquely impacted the family which has been stripped of many of its defenses and disengaged from the larger context of kinship and the extended family. Furthermore, as Peter and Bridget Berger have rightly observed, the family has also been invaded by the outside world by the "experts" and external authorities that now presume to define the inner life of the family on behalf of the larger culture. Vast changes with respect to authority have also marked this culture shift. The old sources of authority—including the church, parents, and teachers—have been replaced by an army of knowledge workers, welfare agencies, and legal entanglements. Furthermore, the digital revolution has added an unprecedented multiplication of these trends so that we have actually entered a time in which, on many important issues, it is the teenager who may have superior expertise to their parents. At no previous time in human history has this been the case, much less common. These intellectual and cultural changes set the stage for our society's deconstruction of marriage.

Four Leading Factors/Precursors to the Same-Sex Revolution

Long before those in same-sex relationships had any realistic hope for the legal recognition of their unions, heterosexuals in the modern age were accomplishing the weakening and structural compromise of marriage all on their own. Any consideration of the eclipse of marriage in the last century must take into consideration four massive developments: birth control and contraception, divorce, advanced reproductive technologies, and cohabitation.

Birth Control and Contraception

The arrival of modern contraception changed human history, and the sexual revolution was fueled by the separation of sex from procreation. It was the availability of birth control in a reliable form, made possible by the development of the Pill, that unleashed the sexual revolution. So long as sex was predictably related to the potential of pregnancy, a huge biological check on sex outside of marriage functioned as a barrier to sexual immorality. Once that barrier was removed, sex and children became effectively separated and sex became redefined as an activity that did not have any necessary relation to the gift of children. It is *impossible* to exaggerate the importance of the separation of sex and babies from the moral equation.

Though a number of evangelicals simply consider birth control and contraceptive technology to be features of the modern age that can be used without much moral or biblical reflection, the use of birth control was historically condemned by every single Christian denomination until the twentieth century. In the United States, most Protestant denominations resisted the temptation to endorse birth control and contraception—for a while. One major development in the Christian conversation took place when Pope Paul VI released his encyclical *Humanae Vitae* in 1968. The Pope definitively closed the door on any artificial birth control. In response, evangelicals seemed to be thankful that they had no Pope to make such a declaration. Most seemed to think that birth control was a Roman Catholic preoccupation and that they should not understand contraception to come with any urgent theological or moral questions. And yet, it was evangelicals, not Roman Catholics, who were stepping outside of the Christian mainstream when it came to approving artificial birth control.

In more recent years, many evangelicals have begun to reconsider the morality of birth control and contraception and, on the positive side, have come to affirm the unconditional goodness of the gift of children. However, the lack of serious evangelical engagement with the arrival of birth control set the stage for evangelical failure on an even larger level, and that failure is tied to the issue of divorce.

Divorce

Like birth control, divorce was inconceivable for most Christians throughout the history of the Christian church. Where it was legally available, it was under the most restrictive conditions in which some guilt (usually adultery) had to be assigned to one party or the other. That would, on credible legal grounds, justify a divorce. The complicated and often excruciating legal processes for obtaining a divorce were intended to make a point about the value of marriage and the disaster that every marital breakup represents—"the death of a small civilization."[27] However, as the twentieth century dawned, theories of sexual liberation and developments in the law began to point toward a potential loosening of the restrictions on legal divorce. The climax of those developments was the first *no-fault* divorce law, signed into effect by then Governor Ronald Reagan in California in 1969.

Regrettably, if the society failed with the challenge of divorce, the Christian church failed even more inexcusably. Many factors were behind this failure. In the same way that so many secular authorities had argued for no-fault divorce as a way of overcoming the hypocrisy of the older system of divorce law, many Christians began to advocate the abandonment of biblical church discipline because of the hypocrisy that sometimes corrupted that process. But destroying marriage is too high a price to pay for avoiding the risk of hypocrisy.

Another factor was the close alignment of Christianity and cultural Christianity. From a theological perspective, the problem of cultural Christianity is that the culture always predominates over the Christianity. Divorce became a prime example of the fact that when the culture lost its mind on marriage, far too many churches decided to join the irrationality. Thus, evangelical churches began to treat divorce as a non-issue, even as the Bible includes the strongest statements imaginable about the permanence of marriage and the sinfulness of divorce. God declared that He "hates" divorce (Mal. 2:16 NASB). Ultimately, the evangelical abdication of responsibility for divorce set the stage for of a loss of evangelical credibility to speak to the larger issue of sexuality and marriage.

Advanced Reproductive Technologies

Another major social shift with huge moral consequences was the development of advanced reproductive technologies. In one sense, this is the parallel development to contraception. If the arrival of birth control separated sex from procreation, the arrival of advanced reproductive technologies separated procreation from sex. The influence of advanced reproductive technologies on the sexual revolution is enormous. These technologies allow persons who are biologically unable to have children to "have" children by some other means. It has enabled same-sex couples and single persons to "have" children, but not by moral means of procreation.

Once again, we need to understand that this revolution affected moral judgments and convictions far beyond those who were actually employing or considering the employment of these advanced reproductive technologies. The arrival of these technologies redefined the very notion of what it meant to "have" a baby for all persons living in advanced nations. Until the most recent period, "having" a baby required a man and a woman in the act of sex. Babies were inseparable from the marital act and, as millennia of human experience demonstrated, having sex meant having babies.

But the redefinition of all relationships was driven by the knowledge that sex between a man and woman was now no longer necessary in order to produce a child. By the second decade of the twenty-first century, the combination of in-vitro fertilization, donor insemination, a commercial gamete market for sperm and eggs, and pervasive availability of surrogate motherhood, allowed persons, single and coupled, heterosexual and homosexual, to "have" a child.

Cohabitation: Sex Outside of Marriage

In previous centuries, non-marital cohabitation between a man and a woman was not only frowned upon, it was sometimes even illegal. Furthermore, most societies found a way of turning lasting cohabitating unions into some form of marriage. Additionally, sex outside of marriage was so morally sanctioned that the revelation of premarital or extramarital sex almost immediately led to grief, guilt, and the censure of society. But, even as society grew weary of divorce and birth control, it grew weary of policing sex outside of marriage as well. Marriage has been established as the norm, the expectation, the mark of adulthood, and as the only socially appropriate context for sexual intercourse and procreation. All that has changed.

Within the first decade of the twenty-first century, rates of extramarital sex and cohabitation had risen to levels experienced by no previous human society. Many Americans now live with marriage completely off their radar. By 2012, the *New York Times* reported that for "women under age 30, most births now occur outside of marriage."[28] The *Times* also reported, "Among mothers of all ages, a majority—59 percent in 2009—are married when they have children. But the surge of births outside marriage among younger women—nearly two-thirds of children in the United States are born to mothers under 30—is both a symbol of the transforming family and a hint of coming generational change."[29]

In a final observation about the lack of moral sanction against sex outside of marriage, we simply have to note the tremendous shift on the sinfulness of adultery that is taking place in America at large. Throughout the centuries, adultery was not only seen as sinful, it was considered a crime. These days, adultery drives popular culture and entertainment, and it fuels the breakup of countless marital unions. The sexual revolution could never have gained the type of traction it has in the culture if adultery had continued to be understood as a great evil to be avoided and a sin to be sanctioned.

Taken together, these four features of the modern age undermined marriage before the culture ever started down the path of the normalization of homosexuality and the legalization of same-sex marriage. The modern age's rapid subversion of marriage in the twentieth century is simply unprecedented. In very powerful words, Tom W. Smith, director of the General Social Survey of the National Opinion Research Center at the University of Chicago, cuts right to the heart of the matter: "What we've seen is a massive change in one generation, a change that is so great that the majority of parents of young children today were raised in a different type of family than they live in today."[30]

The marriage crisis is a moral crisis. It did not start with same-sex marriage, nor will it end there. This has all been made possible by a deliberate breakdown in the moral immune system of human society. Western civilization has forfeited its immunity against the breakdown of marriage, the family, and the integrity of human sexuality. We sowed the seeds of the current confusion. To make matters infinitely worse, the failure of Christian churches to address these issues with the full weight of Christian conviction has created, in the eyes of many, an insurmountable challenge to evangelical credibility on the issue of homosexuality and same-sex marriage. Today's movement toward the total acceptance of homosexual behavior and relationships was only made possible because some heterosexuals first did their best to undermine marriage.

The Same-Sex Revolution

Polling demonstrates that as recently as 2008 the majority of Americans affirmed that they believed homosexual behavior was immoral and homosexual relationships were unworthy of legal recognition of marriage. By 2014, numerous polls indicated a vast shift in the American population on this issue. These polls show a majority of Americans now support the legalization of same-sex marriage. This reversal in a society's collective moral judgment is staggering. How did this happen.

Linda Hirshman's *Victory: The Triumphant Gay Revolution* documents the outworking of the homosexual agenda's progress. As she argues, the public acceptance of homosexuality had to overcome the "four horsemen" of moral judgment. Those arguing for the normalization of homosexuality had to overcome the pervasive judgment in America that homosexuals were "crazy, sinful, criminal, and subversive."[31]

Hirshman's first section—*crazy*—notes that until the early 1970s both the American Psychiatric Association and the American Psychological Association held that same-sex attraction was a form of mental illness. Historian David Eisenbach explains that activists within the American Psychiatric Association used the tactic known as the "zap" to shut down any meeting, conference, or assembly they deemed hostile to their cause. As a result, and as Hirshman makes clear, the APA reversed its judgment on homosexuality. Now one of the preeminent intellectual forces in American public life, the therapeutic profession, now functions as a reliable ally for the normalization of homosexuality. In fact, in American popular culture, to consider homosexuality to be morally suspect, in any way, or a form of mental illness is culturally dismissed. "Homophobia" is now the new mental illness and moral deficiency, while homosexuality is accepted as the new normal. Ultimately, the social acceptance of homosexuality could not have happened if psychiatrists and psychologists were committed to labeling homosexuality a disease.

Hirshman's second category—*sinful*—reflects that in the mid-twentieth century cultural Christianity and its moral judgments were dominant in American culture. The normalization of same-sex relationships and behaviors could not have happened without a significant group of liberal religious leaders who were willing to declare that the church's position on the sinfulness of homosexuality was in error. As Hirshman explains, "[churches] are part of the unofficial apparatus of social approval, so central to the gay revolution."[32] Without the cooperation of at least some leaders and churches within organized Christianity, it is hard to say that the homosexual movement could have proved so successful over the last several decades.

The third of Hirshman's categories—*criminal*—points to the reality that some states still criminalized homosexual acts and behaviors, even as recently as 2003. A succession of cases that demonstrates the moral and legal revolution in America's highest court reveals the significant role the Supreme Court plays on the issue of homosexuality. In 1986, the Supreme Court ruled that the state of Georgia was not violating the Constitution by criminalizing sodomy. Just ten years later, the court's ruling in *Romer v. Evans* decided that no state law targeting those with a same-sex sexual orientation could be constitutional. In 2003, *Lawrence v. Texas* ruled that all laws criminalizing sodomy violated the United States Constitution.

Finally, in June 2013, the court struck down the Defense of Marriage Act (DOMA) which Congress had passed in 1998 after the state of Hawaii haltingly moved toward the adoption of legal same-sex marriage. DOMA declared that the federal government would recognize marriage only as the union of a man and a woman, and that no state would be forced by the Commerce Clause of the Constitution to legally recognize a same-sex marriage performed in any other state. The *Windsor* decision's decisive strike down of DOMA immediately led to a host of changes in policy, law, and the affairs of our entire governmental system. Then, in June 2015, the Supreme Court's *Obergefell* ruling brought the legal battle over same-sex marriage to a climactic end, an end whose full consequences are yet unknown. Revolutions in the culture and revolution in the law are inseparable. The courts are an indispensable battlefield and function as an ally to the sexual revolutionaries, just as they have in any other movement that has forced massive structural and moral change in American society.

The last of Linda Hirshman's "four horsemen" is the perception that homosexuality is *subversive* to the moral order. The effort to normalize same-sex relationships has succeeded most when it presents homosexuals as harmless neighbors, kind-hearted friends, and contributing members of a happy society. The nation's entertainment culture has provided writers Kirk and Madsen's strategy the space it needed to thrive. A concerted effort to present a constant parade of happy, nonthreatening homosexuals in popular culture has undercut the notion that homosexuality is subversive to a healthy society.

In the December 1984 issue of the gay publication *Christopher Street*, Marshall Kirk joined Erastes Pill (a pseudonym for Hunter

Madsen) to write "Waging Peace: A Gay Battle Plan to Persuade Straight America." In that article, Kirk and Pill wrote:

> Where we talk is important. The visual media, film and television, are plainly the most powerful image-makers in Western civilization. The average American household watches over seven hours of TV daily. Those hours open up a gateway into the private world of straights, through which a Trojan horse might be passed. As far as desensitization is concerned, the medium is the message—of normalcy. So far, gay Hollywood has provided our best covert weapon in the battle to desensitize the mainstream. Bit by bit over the past ten years, gay characters and gay themes have been introduced into TV programs and films. . . . On the whole, the impact has been encouraging.[33]

As veteran media analyst Michael Medved argues, the effort to push this agenda in Hollywood has been devastatingly effective—largely because no equally concentrated and invested strategy to defend marriage is present in mainstream media. Referring to the article by Kirk and Pill, Medved observes: "Hearing the agenda outlined so brilliantly in this article, can anyone doubt that part of the problem, in what some people have called the culture war, is that one side is prepared and organized and determined, and the other side is just gradually beginning to wake up?"[34]

Conclusion

The sexual revolution presents a monumental challenge to the Christian church, but the church has faced great challenges before. These are not the first revolutionary times that have demanded a Christian response—as those who have been dispersed throughout the world. The New Testament implies that all Christians in all times are, in some sense, exiles. The New Testament church came as an exile into the polytheistic paganism of first-century Rome. The apostle Peter addressed these first-century Christians as resident aliens (1 Pet. 1:1; 2:11). The Epistle to Diognetus, one of the earliest Christian writings, describes Christians as those who have no home and yet are at home everywhere.

In this new age, however, the church faces a revolution different than those of the past. As we have seen, this moral revolution challenges the very heart of Christian conviction and faithfulness. We have also seen that this revolution did not erupt out of a vacuum. Decades of intellectual shift and social change preceded this revolution and made it possible, if not inevitable. Furthermore, we must recognize that as the sexual revolution gains more and more traction in the court of public opinion, the church will continue to be displaced in the larger culture.

Christians must now choose between cultural retreat and isolation or reformation and gospel engagement. As Christians we may live in exile in the world, but exile does not mean the end of Christian witness or Christian faithfulness. As the apostle Peter taught, Christians are "a chosen race, a royal priesthood, a holy nation, a people for his own possession, that you may proclaim the excellencies of him who called you out of darkness into his marvelous light" (1 Pet. 2:9). Fidelity to Christ in this generation demands that we open our mouths and our lives to the world and bear witness to Christ as those committed to the authority of Scripture, the sanctity of marriage, and to the gospel of the Lord Jesus. Christians may find themselves in exile but the gospel they preach is never in retreat.

Discussion Questions

1. In what ways does a biblical theology of sexuality contradict secular attitudes about sexuality?
2. What kinds of opportunities exist for the church when its teachings on sexuality fall out of favor in culture?
3. How should Christians who find themselves at odds with the culture over sexuality and same-sex marriage communicate a biblical understanding of marriage?

ADDITIONAL READING

Is God Anti-Gay? And Other Questions about Homosexuality, the Bible, and Same-Sex Attraction by Sam Allberry

What Does the Bible Really Teach about Homosexuality? by Kevin DeYoung

The Secret Thoughts of an Unlikely Convert by Rosaria Butterfield

Washed and Waiting: Reflections on Christian Faithfulness and Homosexuality by Wesley Hill

Ministry in the New Marriage Culture by Jeff Iorg

Marriage Is: How Marriage Transforms Society and Cultivates Human Flourishing by Andrew T. Walker and Eric Teetsel

The Meaning of Marriage: Facing the Complexities of Commitment with the Wisdom of God by Timothy Keller

What's the Difference? Manhood and Womanhood Defined According to the Bible by John Piper

Sex, Romance, and the Glory of God: What Every Christian Needs to Know by C. J. Mahaney

We Cannot Be Silent: Speaking Truth to a Culture Redefining Sex, Marriage, and the Very Meaning of Right and Wrong by R. Albert Mohler Jr.

ACKNOWLEDGMENTS

TO THE MANY HANDS INSIDE AND OUTSIDE THE ERLC, WE THANK you for your help and assistance on this book. The ERLC team provided joyful encouragement in the planning and execution of this series, and without them, it would never have gotten off the ground. We want to also personally thank Phillip Bethancourt who was a major visionary behind this project. We'd also like to thank Jennifer Lyell and Devin Maddox at B&H, our publisher, for their work in guiding us through this process. We'd also like to thank the administrative teams of J. D. Greear, Albert Mohler, and John Piper for assisting in this project.

ABOUT THE ERLC

THE ERLC IS DEDICATED TO ENGAGING THE CULTURE WITH the gospel of Jesus Christ and speaking to issues in the public square for the protection of religious liberty and human flourishing. Our vision can be summed up in three words: kingdom, culture, and mission.

Since its inception, the ERLC has been defined around a holistic vision of the kingdom of God, leading the culture to change within the church itself and then as the church addresses the world. The ERLC has offices in Washington, DC, and Nashville, Tennessee.

ABOUT THE CONTRIBUTORS

Jason G. Duesing is provost and associate professor of Historical Theology at Midwestern Baptist Theological Seminary and College in Kansas City, Missouri.

J. D. Greear, PhD is pastor of The Summit Church in Raleigh-Durham, North Carolina.

R. Albert Mohler Jr. serves as president of The Southern Baptist Theological Seminary in Louisville, Kentucky.

John Piper speaks and writes regularly through Desiring God. He also serves as Chancellor of Bethlehem College and Seminary in Minneapolis, Minnesota.

Andrew T. Walker serves as director of Policy Studies with The Ethics & Religious Liberty Commission.

NOTES

1. Sherif Girgis, Ryan T. Anderson, and Robert P. George, *What Is Marriage? Man and Woman: A Defense* (New York: Encounter Books, 2012).

2. Quote attributed to Susan Sontag.

3. Paul Rampell, "A High Divorce Rate Means It's Time to Try 'Wedleases,'" *Washington Post*, August 4, 2013, http://www.washingtonpost.com/opinions/a-high-divorce-rate-means-its-time-to-try-wedleases/2013/08/04/f2221c1c-f89e-11e2-b018-5b8251f0c56e_story.html.

4. Mark Oppenheimer, "Dan Savage on the Virtues of Infidelity," *New York Times*, June 30, 2011, http://www.nytimes.com/2011/07/03/magazine/infidelity-will-keep-us-together.html.

5. Molly Young, "He & He & He," *NYMag.com*, July 29, 2012, http://nymag.com/news/features/benny-morecock-throuple.

6. "Redefine Marriage, Debase Language?," *National Review Online*, accessed April 24, 2015, http://www.nationalreview.com/article/355295/redefine-marriage-debase-language-ryan-t-anderson.

7. Girgis, Anderson, and George, *What Is Marriage?*, 10.

8. Ibid., 10–11.

9. Russell D. Moore, "Man, Woman, and the Mystery of Christ: An Evangelical Protestant Perspective," *Journal of the Evangelical Theological Society* 58, no. 1 (March 2015): 89–94.

10. This idea is attributed to the work of Maggie Gallagher.

11. Popular revisionist accounts can be seen in the work of Matthew Vines, *God and the Gay Christian* (New York: Convergent Books, 2014); David Gushee, *Changing Our Mind* (Canton, MI: David Crumm Media, LLC, 2014). For interaction and rebuttal of these books, see Andrew T. Walker, "Reformation or Revolution: A Review of God and the Gay Christian," *Canon and Culture*, http://www.canonandculture.com/reformation-or-revolution-a-review-of-god-and-the-gay-christian; R. Albert Mohler Jr., ed., *God and the Gay Christian?: A Response to Matthew Vines* (SBTS Press, 2014); George Guthrie, "Changing Our Mind," *The Gospel Coalition*, January 9, 2015, http://www.thegospelcoalition.org/article/changing-our-mind.

12. Robert A. J. Gagnon, *The Bible and Homosexual Practice: Texts and Hermeneutics* (Nashville: Abingdon Press, 2001), 306–31.

13. *WORLD Magazine*, June 16, 2012, 108.

14. "So What Is This 'Keep Calm and Carry On' Thing All About Then?" at http://www.keepcalmandcarryon.com/history.

15. Carl F. H. Henry, *The Uneasy Conscience of Modern Fundamentalism* (Wheaton: Crossway, [1947], 2003), 53–55.

16. Ibid., 25.

17. Martyn Lloyd-Jones, *I Am Not Ashamed: Advice to Timothy* (Grand Rapids: Baker, 1986), 15.

18. Ibid., 33.

19. John Calvin, *Commentaries on the Epistles to Timothy, Titus, and Philemon* (Grand Rapids: Baker, 2003), 179.

20. Such is the suggestion of A. T. Robertson in his *Word Pictures in the New Testament: The Epistles of Paul*, Vol. 4 (Nashville: Broadman, 1931), 612.

21. Mark Dever, "Condemned Sin: Romans 8:1–4" and Michael Lawrence, *It Is Well: Expositions on Substitutionary Atonement* (Wheaton: Crossway, 2010), 169.

22. William Cowper, "God Moves in a Mysterious Way" in John Newton, *Olney Hymns in Three Books* (London, 1824), 199–200.

23. Carl F. H. Henry, *Confessions of a Theologian* (Waco: Word, 1986), 390.

24. P. P. Bliss, "It Is Well with My Soul," in Ira David Sankey and P. P. Bliss, *Gospel Hymns,* No. 2 (Cincinnati: John Church, 1895), 412. See also Lloyd-Jones' use of this in *I Am Not Ashamed*, 20.

25. Theo Hobson, "A Pink Reformation," *The Guardian*, February 2007, http://www.theguardian.com/commentisfree/2007/feb/05/apink reformation.

26. Ibid.

27. Pat Conroy, "Anatomy of a Divorce," *Atlanta*, November 1, 1978, http://www.atlantamagazine.com/great-reads/anatomy-of-a-divorce.

28. Jason DeParle and Sabrina Tavernise, "For Women Under 30, Most Births Occur Outside Marriage," *New York Times*, February 17, 2012, http://www.nytimes.com/2012/02/18/us/for-women-under-30-most-births-occur-outside-marriage.html. Two days after the publication of that report, the same newspaper declared that "out-of-wedlock births are the new normal" for younger mothers. See KJ Dell'Antonia, "For Younger Mothers, Out-of-Wedlock Births Are the New Normal," *New York Times*, February 19, 2012, http://parenting.blogs.nytimes.com/2012/02/19/for-younger-mothers-out-of-wedlock-births-are-the-new-normal.

29. Ibid.

30. Tom W. Smith in "Where Are We and How Did We Get Here?," in *Marriage—Just a Piece of Paper?*, eds. Katherine Anderson, Don Browning, and Brian Boyer (Grand Rapids: Wm. B. Eerdmans Publishing, 2002), 26.

31. Linda Hirshman, *Victory: The Triumphant Gay Revolution* (New York: Harper Perennial, 2013), 129.

32. Ibid., 145.

33. Quoted in Michael Medved, "Homosexuality and the Entertainment Media," *New Oxford Review*, Vol. 68, No. 6 (June 2001): 37.

34. Ibid.